The
SOLITARY
WAR
of a
SNIPER

The SOLITARY WAR of a SNIPER

THE AUTHORISED BIOGRAPHY OF
BRITAIN'S MOST SUCCESSFUL WORLD WAR II SNIPER

by
Martin Pegler

Greenhill Books

The Solitary War of a British Sniper

First published in 2025 by
Greenhill Books,
c/o Pen & Sword Books Ltd,
George House, Unit 12 & 13,
Beevor Street, Off Pontefract Road,
Barnsley, South Yorkshire S71 1HN

www.greenhillbooks.com
contact@greenhillbooks.com

ISBN: 978–1–80500–119–5
ePub ISBN 978–1–80500–120–1
pdf ISBN 978–1–80500–121–8

© Martin Pegler, 2025

All rights reserved. No part of this book may be reproduced,
transmitted, downloaded, decompiled or reverse engineered
in any form or by any means, electronic or mechanical
including photocopying, recording or by any information storage
and retrieval system, without permission from the Publisher in writing.
No part of this book may be used or reproduced in any manner
for the purpose of training artificial intelligence technologies or systems.

The right of Martin Pegler to be identified as author of this work
has been asserted in accordance with Section 77
of the Copyrights, Designs and Patents Act 1988.

CIP data records for this title are available from the British Library

The Publisher's authorised representative in the EU
for product safety is Authorised Rep Compliance Ltd.,
Ground Floor, 71 Lower Baggot Street, Dublin D02 P593, Ireland.
www.arccompliance.com

Edited and designed by Donald Sommerville
Typeset in 12/14.5 pt. Adobe Garamond Pro
and 10.5/14 Myriad Pro Light

Printed and bound in the UK by CPI Group (UK) Ltd,
Croydon, CR0 4YY

Frontispiece: Musketry Sergeant Harry Furness, in a studio photograph taken in 1946. His shoulder patch shows the 49th Division Polar Bear. Below that, unofficially, he wears the cap badge of the Yorks and Lancs Regiment above his crossed rifles sniper qualification, which was normally worn on the left sleeve although never in combat. He also sports his treasured Omega watch.

Contents

	List of Plates and Illustrations	ix
	Acknowledgements	xi
	Preface	xiii
Chapter 1	Learning the Trade	1
Chapter 2	Sniper Training and Equipment	8
Chapter 3	D-Day and Into the *Bocage*	58
Chapter 4	Driving Inland	72
Chapter 5	Belgium and the Netherlands	108
Chapter 6	Aftermath and Later Life	141
Chapter 7	Reflections	157
Appendix 1	The Enfield No. 4 (T) Sniping Rifle	160
Appendix 2	Specifications	180
	Notes	181
	Bibliography	187
	Index	188

Dedication

To the generation who lived through
the greatest war in human history,
and sacrificed so much in order that
we might enjoy what they did not.

Plates and Illustrations

Plates

Sergeant H. M Furness in May 1945; Harry's family just before the war (*both AR*).

Captain Underhill lecturing to trainee snipers (*HMF*); a sniper in training, wearing a Patt. 1943 Smock (*Author*).

Canadian snipers in full ghillie suits; a German machine-gun crew and sniper team (*both Author*).

Canadians landing on Juno Beach on D-Day (*Canadian War Memorial*); an aerial view of *bocage* country (*HMF*).

Commandos and a Sherman tank near Sword Beach (*HMF*); a Churchill Mk VII 'Crocodile' (*Tank Museum, Bovington*); MG 42 machine gun and crew (*Bundesarchiv*).

Harry's 'No. 2 rifle' (*Author*); 2nd Pattern Fairbairn-Sykes knife carried by Harry (*Courtesy Nigel Greenaway*); Harry's 'Case, Tel. No. 8 1941' (*Author*).

A platoon of the Hallamshires, July 1944 (*IWM B5645*); Sherman 'Rhino' hedge-cutter in Caen (*HMF*).

A sniper-scouting patrol in the *bocage* (*HMF*); Sniper James Donald, KOSB, Holland, late 1944 (*Author*).

A 6-pounder anti-tank gun, Willemstad, November, 1944 (*HMF*); Kangaroo troop carrier (*Tank Museum, Bovington*).

A Nebelwerfer 41 being reloaded (*Bundesarchiv*); Black Watch sniper in a roof hide in Gennep, Holland (*Author*).

Nijmegen Bridge shortly after its capture (*Author*); Buffalo amphibians unloading (*Tank Museum, Bovington*).

British sniper in a snowsuit (*Author*); Churchill Crab flail tank, Arnhem, 15 April 1944 (*Tank Museum, Bovington*).

Harry during the shooting championships at Haltern; one of the first photos Harry took of Erni; Harry in Berlin; Harry and Erni's wedding day (*all HMF*).

Harry and his cameras in the late 1970s (*HMF*); Harry and his brother John, in uniform post-war (*AR*); Harry and Erni (*AR*); the couple's final resting place (*AR*).

Harry and his 'No. 2' sniping rifle in 2004 (*Author*).

Illustrations in Text

Harry's childhood home (*Courtesy Google Streetview*)	page 3
How camouflage should work (*both HMF*)	16, 17
A 'Complete Equipment Schedule' case (*Former Sniper Sergeant B. Lees photo*)	23
The view through Harry's No. 32 Mk II sight (*Author*)	27
A very early 1st Pattern Denison Smock (*Courtesy JM Militaria Collection, Haaksbergen, Netherlands*)	41
The German sniper Bruno Sutkus (*Wikimedia Commons*)	68
A sergeant cleaning the rifle of a sleeping sniper (*HMF*)	77
The Depôt de Mendicité (*HMF*)	110
A German with a Panzerfaust 60 (*Bundesarchiv*)	113
Hallamshires and a DUKW, near Zetten (*IWM 15021*)	133
Liberated civilians, Ellecom, April 1944 (*IWM BU 3630*)	138
Harry's post-war uniform (*Author*)	143
Harry and his Leica in the late 1950s (*HMF*)	155
Stock wrist and bolt of Harry's No. 2 rifle (*Author*)	165
The scope mounting on Harry's No. 2 rifle (*Author*)	170

Source Abbreviations: HMF = Harry Mitchell Furness; AR = Annette Ryan.

Acknowledgements

FIRSTLY, I OFFER MY GRATEFUL THANKS to Harry's daughter, Annette and her husband Martin. Annette very generously provided access to Harry's personal documents as well as previously unseen photographs, and patiently answered my innumerable questions about her father's earlier life. And in no particular order, my thanks to Nigel Greenaway for checking the early text and contributing photographs of Harry's knife, Dr Roger Payne, whose knowledge of the technicalities of the Enfield No. 4 (T) is unsurpassed and who clarified many of the finer technical points. Jordy, in Holland who holds a remarkable collection of WW2 uniforms (https://jmmilitaria.com) and who kindly photographed one of his Denison smocks for me. I am indebted to Andrew Webb, at the Image and Film Department at the Imperial War Museum, for the Hallamshire images, and of course, to John Walter for his patient, precise and very helpful editing of the text.

A big thank-you goes to Martin Windrow, a living legend in the publishing world, for helping to guide me in the right direction, enabling me eventually to begin work on this book. Then to my ever-patient wife Katie, who once more accepted my disappearance for hours on end while I worked on the book, and for helping enormously by reading, editing and cross-referencing twenty-plus years of correspondence with Harry. Finally, to Michael Leventhal of Greenhill Books who has waited very patiently for this manuscript to appear.

Notes Regarding Images

Harry's childhood was not particularly well documented in print or photographically and I am indebted to Annette for her detective work in finding the one surviving family image that I have used. With regard to the many purported 'sniping' photos taken during the war, I should point out that with a couple of very rare exceptions, virtually every published image of a sniper was posed for the camera. No sniper would ever consent to having an untrained photographer lugging a camera with him on a patrol, as it would be a death sentence for all concerned. There do exist a very few images of the Hallamshires in action and as several of these relate directly to Harry's account of events, they have been selected. It was also unusual for so many late-war pictures to be taken of an individual soldier such as Harry, but he was of particular interest to the Army Film and Photographic Unit (AFPU) whose official photographers chose him for several press portraits. This was because his renown (he would have hated the word 'fame') as a sniper within the army was irrefutable. He personally accumulated a considerable photographic archive and most of these were annotated by him, so despite some being of rather average quality, I have reproduced a few of them with his comments, where relevant.

Preface

WHEN I WAS FIRST PUT IN TOUCH WITH HARRY, it took several months before he agreed to see me, having first thoroughly checked on my credentials as a trustworthy author. This, I subsequently realised, was typical of his methodical and patient approach to everything he undertook, and it was the underlying reason he survived as a combat sniper. I knew him for over twenty years and we developed a firm friendship, based on a totally unrealistic basis. I said he was the best sniper in the world and he thought I was the best sniping author. Neither was true, of course. Although initially he would talk happily about the technicalities of sniping and training, it took much longer before he felt comfortable enough with me to begin discussing his war on a more personal level. The one factor about which he remained consistent was his adamant refusal to allow me to write his biography. He was an intensely private man and his primary concern was that nothing should ever be written that could in any way affect his wife and daughter, both of whom he adored. Although he did permit some anecdotes to be used in a few books, both mine and by other authors, I reluctantly accepted that his biography would probably remain unwritten. When he died, Annette surprised me by forwarding an email, that in his final days he never managed to send, informing me that after his death I had his blessing finally to write his biography. To aid in this project, he also left me a considerable quantity of personal papers and copies of all the correspondence we had ever had between us.

This was quite a challenge to me, as all of my writing to date has been based on weapon technology or military history. A biography is very a different form of authorship and after some considerable time-wasting I was advised that it would be both pointless and confusing for a reader to have a biography that was not set in any proper chronological context. So, while this book is primarily about one man's war and his experiences, thoughts and fears, for the sake of clarity it has been placed in an overall military–historical framework.

However, the last thing I wanted to do was to write yet another history of D-Day, as many professional historians with a far greater understanding of those events have competently done this. If the reader wants to delve deeper into this aspect, then the bibliography will provide the means to do so. So, while the overall strategy of operations surrounding Harry's service is mentioned, the core of this book is based around an overview of the events that embroiled the two regiments he saw combat with: briefly the Green Howards (Alexandra, Princess of Wales's Own Yorkshire Regiment) and then his far longer time with the Hallamshires (the Hallamshire Battalion, York and Lancaster Regiment). So this biography could perhaps be likened to a set on stage, the battlefields of North-Western Europe being the backdrop in which the main actor, Corporal, later Sergeant Furness, makes frequent appearances. In fact, Harry did write an account of his war for use in Don Scott's excellent history *Polar Bears From Sheffield*, but only small numbers of his anecdotes were used where space permitted, as much of his manuscript proved far too detailed for such a generic historical publication. Thus, it remained as a hand-typed text of seventy pages, a copy of which he gave to me many years ago. As far as I am aware, Harry is unique as the only serving British sniper ever to write any form of detailed account about his war, but as he pointed out in his memoir:

> I would like to make it clear that my notes are in not in any way meant to represent a history of snipers at war, that is best left to those eminently better qualified to do so. My personal notes are memories only of one who served in the ranks and naturally saw our wartime activities from an entirely different viewpoint, so full allowance must be made for that fact. Right after my demobilisation from the army I did start to write down details of those events while they were still fresh in my mind, for I was still so full

of it all and was finding it hard to re-settle into civilian life after all I had gone through in the front line as a sniper. It was never my intention to put it into book form for others to read; it was just an attempt to get it out of my system. But my family wanted me to put it all behind me … so my notes with dates and places and times were all burnt. Now writing these notes some 49 years later [i.e. *c*.1997] the details of where and at what time and at what date certain events happened are no longer quite clear … but the actual incidents were so dramatic to me that until this day much of it remains quite clear in my mind, and no doubt will remain with me until my death. Wartime experiences in which your life is at stake do not fade away. Perhaps the horror and grim reality of it mellow with time, but the memories never leave you.

Certainly, former snipers may not be too keen to recall the macabre memories in which they themselves took part, for most of us have since pushed these grimmer memories from our minds since that time, [and] even now hesitate to bring them up once more. Those of us who took part were under heavy stress (although as a matter of pride we didn't allow it to be seen at the time) but for many it showed up later in civilian life in various forms of illness and few were spared these much later stress-related problems.

The majority of what follows in these pages is based around Harry's memoir, but in addition we exchanged dozens of letters over nearly twenty years, for he was a very zealous correspondent, and I also made notes about specific questions during visits to see him. At times I must have seemed like a secretary rather than a friend, but my previous experience of interviewing Great War veterans was that if I did not record everything I could at the time, it would be lost for ever. These notes have fortunately provided a wealth of information, some of it very detailed indeed. However, none of this was in any chronological order whatsoever and it has taken a great deal of work to try and match up events with places and dates through other published sources – not always, I will admit, to my complete satisfaction.

Wherever possible, I have used Harry's own words to convey the information, feelings and drama of his tiny part in a huge war and these are always printed in a different font so they are clearly identified as quotations. Many quotations include his personal opinions, which may not always be in accordance with historical facts. Harry's text has not been edited in any material way but minor mis-spellings and obvious typing errors have been silently corrected. All italic type used in quoted text represents emphasis that Harry marked in the originals. Words or phrases in quotes that are placed in [square brackets] are editorial additions. Harry naturally used imperial units of measurement in his accounts; the editorial text in this book follows his example in all technical contexts.

Snipers are by nature reticent and self-effacing men and Harry more so than many. He did not glory in war or killing and in later life had many misgivings about the role he played, but, as he pointed out:

> I was trained to do a very specific job, and I did it as professionally as I could. Every German soldier I killed was one less to take the life of a British soldier, and even if it wasn't always appreciated at the time, I regarded my job as saving the lives of my comrades. I did not allow myself to brood over what had to be done which had to end with the death or disablement of another soldier, and nor did I ever attempt to calculate possible tallies, which I find meaningless.

These memoirs inevitably bring one to the rather thorny subject of his total tally, which I have been asked about frequently. It is on record that it was in excess of 100, but the actual figure he told me I promised never to divulge. It should be borne in mind, though, that 'official' kills take into account *only* those shots that were witnessed by an independent observer, and recorded at the time. The majority of Harry's sniping was done on his own, far from British lines, or in the heat of combat when there was no time to dwell on whether a particular shot had killed the intended target or not. As he said, it was of no consequence to him anyway. He had a job to do and he did it as efficiently as possible, although he was very specific about the subject of recording kills.

Preface

> We never discussed kills within our section or with other infantrymen. A POW, when first captured, is in fear of his life and liable to give away valuable information, perhaps unwittingly. So, if the details are not discussed by our snipers, then nothing can be given away by others. Snipers *do not* discuss numbers killed or wounded ... although such details are noted in later log-book entries and discussed with the section Intelligence Officer (IO). The British army does not keep official lists of 'confirmed kills' ... due to the difficulties in being able to definitely confirm such numbers. Other armies are more lax on these requirements, so tallies are suspect.

In particular Harry was very suspicious of the huge numbers of kills reported by Soviet authorities which he believed were mostly the product of journalistic and official propaganda.

In fact, the military service of Sergeant Harry Furness was in many ways little different from that of the tens of thousands of other Allied combat soldiers who took part in the D-Day landings and then slogged their way through France, Belgium, the Netherlands and into Germany. Of course, each soldier's experience was his own and Harry's in a sense even more so, as sniping was so personal. As a battlefield sniper it was little short of miraculous that he survived the war more or less intact. Casualty rates among combat snipers were in excess of 80 per cent killed or wounded in action, and they were considered to be both the most highly trained and also the most vulnerable of all battlefield specialists.

When he returned home in 1947, he was quickly followed by his young German wife, Erni, having rescued both her and her mother from a very uncertain future. Their plan was to apply for a passport for Erni's mum, then bring her to live in Britain, but things did not quite work out as they intended. Harry and Erni remained completely devoted to each other for the rest of their lives and their story alone is a deeply touching reminder that war is all about people. Real, living people who in war sometimes had to kill each other, but also forged lasting friendships and even fell in love. Despite (or perhaps because of) the destruction and grief that the war generated, Harry and Erni were determined to share their lives together, which they did for over seventy years. It has been a matter of great satisfaction and pleasure to me, to put these disparate notes, letters and manuscript memories together into Harry and Erni's story.

I have tried very hard to strike a balance between inserting historical details and giving Harry's own accounts and I hope the reader finds the result interesting, informative and thought-provoking. It has been a labour of love and I am very pleased to have been able to complete it to what I can only hope would be Harry's satisfaction.

Chapter 1

Learning the Trade

FROM THE BRITISH POINT OF VIEW, snipers became an essential, if somewhat repugnant necessity during the Great War of 1914–18, in which by late 1915 on the Western Front they were gradually beginning to establish mastery of no-man's land, dominating the German snipers and taking a heavy toll on the unwary or careless. In 1918, when open warfare broke out, they became a vital part of both the attacking and defending forces, targeting enemy machine guns, officers and NCOs, artillery observers and, of course, opposing snipers. The lessons learned were put into practice as efficient training methods, based on hard-won experience, were taught in the many Sniping Schools established at the time, and were ultimately enshrined in training manuals. Nevertheless, in the 1920s British leaders were either unwilling or unable to bring themselves to continue to train men whose profession had often been described as 'ungentlemanly' during the Great War. It was a curiously antiquated attitude that was to linger within the British Army from the Great War until the 1980s.[1]

Britain's military situation post 1920 was precarious, as the army had been pared down to roughly 275,000 men from the 5 million in uniform at the end of 1918. As was inevitable, defence expenditure had been slashed, the introduction of much-needed new technology was strictly regulated, and training was reduced to a minimum, sufficient only to keep the armed services in a functioning form. This was quite understandable in the face of the monumental debts and human losses created by the First World War. No one, politician or civilian, wanted to consider the possibility of another conflict in Europe. Peace and reconstruction were the watchwords across most of the world and this attitude continued for over a decade, even in the face of increasingly clear evidence after 1933 that Germany was re-arming, despite the restrictions of the Versailles Treaty. Britain was concerned but not unduly worried so did little to convert its still largely Great War-equipped army to a modern footing.

As far as Harry was concerned, the biggest decision that would affect him was the plan to re-design the SMLE rifle, turning it into a more cost-effective and efficient battle weapon that was eventually to become the Rifle, No. 4 Mk I. When he joined up, Harry was not initially issued with this new weapon, as they were in very short supply, so he continued to train with the old SMLE with which he was so familiar from his cadet days. Eventually, though, he came to know the No. 4 rifle more intimately than any infantryman.

Of course, the British government was not entirely blind to what Germany was doing in terms of re-arming during the 1930s, and went to some effort to ensure that when war did happen Britain was as prepared as possible. By 1939 ground radar installations, fast new multi-gun fighter aircraft and heavy bombers had gone some considerable way to offset the military imbalance between the UK and Germany. But there were still almost no facilities for the training of British snipers, and the rifles available were those that had been stored post-1918 and had somehow avoided the great cull of 1923, when the old Rifle, Short, Magazine, Lee-Enfield, Mark III* (SMLE) sniping rifles were stripped of their scopes (which were then sold off to the commercial gun trade). A few still remained in scattered depots as well as several thousand Enfield Pattern 1914 Mk I* W (T) sniping rifles that had been manufactured too late to be issued in the war. The most glaring problem was that even if suitable rifles had existed in any numbers, there were almost no trained men to use them. A few Great War veteran snipers were still in the army, mostly as sergeant instructors, but there was only a single training school at Hythe in Kent and a few individual regiments that had taken it upon themselves to provide basic training. This sad state of affairs continued until the army belatedly realised that a full-scale European war was indeed inevitable, and something must be done very rapidly about the lack of both sniping equipment and men.

It was into this faintly chaotic arena that a young Harry Mitchell Furness unwittingly stepped when he volunteered for military

11 Beresford Street, Salford, Manchester, Harry's family home. No. 9, where his great-aunt lived, is the white door on the left.

service in 1941. What subsequently happened to him provides a unique insight into the training, and the precarious and usually brief life of a combat sniper in Europe in 1944–45. British snipers who survived rarely talked about their experiences and even fewer ever put pen to paper to contribute to the historical record.

Harry was born on 10 March 1925 to John and Jessie Furness. He was their second son, the first, John, being four years older. Harry's family life was unusual by most standards. This was due to his father's profession, for his dad had been a well-known and successful professional bantamweight boxer: John Harold 'Kid' Furness, promoted in the ring as 'The Mighty Atom'. Although by the time of Harry's birth, his father had ceased fighting, John had continued to make boxing his livelihood, becoming a very successful fight promoter. This necessitated the family moving round the country as his father set up travelling boxing rings in much the same manner as an itinerant circus. When they were small the brothers often lived in a travellers' caravan, but they required schooling, of course, so were eventually based in the family home at 11 Beresford Street, Salford, Manchester in the care of 'Aunt' Nellie, the sister of their maternal grandmother, who fortuitously occupied Number 9 next door. Both boys attended Durnford Street School, in Middleton, but little detail has survived about the early school careers of the pair and the school is long gone. Although both were very bright, it appears John was the more studious of the two. Harry loved reading and devoured books all his life, and he became an indefatigable letter-writer, but as a boy he was, according to his daughter, 'a bit of a handful'. He had inherited his father's genes, being of small build, 165 cm / 5 ft 5 in. tall, around 40 kg / 90 lb in weight, endlessly energetic, self-reliant and physically tough. Although he gained some weight as he matured, he was always diminutive. Harry never had much to say about his childhood, but what he did recall as a seminal event was when he joined the school's Army Cadet Force, mostly on the basis of having read and re-read Major H. V. Hesketh-Prichard's book *Sniping in the Great War*.

> As a boy I guess he was my idea of a role-model, so I identified with him and his influence, which certainly led me into the snipers.

He further discovered a useful but hitherto unknown talent for shooting, for it became obvious that he had skills that not everyone possessed. He qualified as a marksman at the age of fourteen, shooting a Great War period .303 in. SMLE rifle (universally and fondly referred to as 'The Smellie'), and proudly pinned the qualification brass crossed rifles onto his battledress. Shooting is both a physical and mental skill and there is no way of determining where this ability comes from in an individual. Harry was simply that one-in-a-thousand who possessed that subtle combination of abilities that coalesced to provide all the requirements for being a skilled shot. Jumping ahead a little, it is unsurprising that in 1940, after he joined what was initially called the Local Defence Volunteers, he was soon appointed company sharpshooter.

One of the very few earlier records about Harry's early life appeared in the war emergency 1939 census under the National Registration Act in a brief entry that stated that his brother was 'a secretary, seeking work' and Harry 'had not been in employment'. As he was fourteen at the time, this is not altogether surprising. In fact he had left school by then and initially went to work as an apprentice with a military tailor in Manchester, called Meggitts. How this might eventually have turned out will never be known, as once his father realised that he was expected to pay for his son's training to complete the apprenticeship, Harry was swiftly removed from Meggitts so he could get proper paid work. Harry's daughter did add, however, that all his life her father retained an interest in clothing and on several occasions tailored his uniforms to fit better. He also liked old furniture[2] and would mend or repair family clothing. But as paid work was the order of the day, he next found a job at Bert Loman's Theatrical Scenery and Stage Supplies Company in central Manchester. There he was trained as a scenic artist and began working on professional stage scenery and became, what he termed:

> … a dab hand at turning what looked like a peasant's cottage into a fairytale castle.
>
> I worked mainly in our very large warehouse facilities as the scenery was all large-scale, and at times when a stage show had badly needed scenery mislaid by the railways, I had to rush down at the last minute to various theatres to re-paint, disguise and alter [scenery] to fit different shows. Sometimes I was still hard at work on stage as the orchestra started playing the opening tunes … working like a madman before the curtain went up. I had a flying start to becoming a good 'camoufleur' … it did affect my view that my deceptive camouflage had to be believable … when I entered action later. Maybe it saved my life?

Despite his enjoyment of the work at Loman's, Harry soon yearned for something much more, and what better way was there to see the world, and perhaps have a little excitement, at someone else's expense, than to join the army? After all, it was obvious by the late 1930s that more men would soon be needed. In Britain, the government had belatedly been forced to react to the threat from Germany: in May 1939 under the Military Training Act, men 20 or 21 years of age were required to register for military service; some 275,000 did so. In September 1939, under the National Service

Act, every able-bodied man of 18–41 years of age had to register. Although still under age, Harry applied to become a boy soldier, so in 1941, at the age of 16, he enlisted in the Princess of Wales's Own Yorkshire Regiment, universally known as the Green Howards. What sort of young soldier he was is open to conjecture as he was never particularly forthcoming on the subject, but his endless energy and the application of steely self-determination must have made him stand out, for he was promoted to boy-corporal within eighteen months. He admitted, though, that he was something of a 'square peg in a round hole' and what he did say was that much of the training, and particularly the square-bashing, he found very irksome. However, he had one ace up his sleeve:

> When we were first taken to the range to fire live ammunition, of course I found it quite easy. Shooting was natural to me and the range sergeant looked at my target and asked when I had learned to shoot. I told him I had qualified as marksman in the Army Cadets. He asked me to fire some more, which I did.

How Harry was to become a sniper is worth explaining here, as the subsequent training he received was to set him on a very different path to the majority of his fellow soldiers and enabled him to wage a personal war that was unique in its function. In early 1941 he heard that the army was forming sniper sections and he at once volunteered.

> The days of being told you were a good shot 'so now you're a sniper' were long gone. All of us were volunteers. The army recognised that unless a man had the right mental attitude and temperament then he would never make a good sniper.

All of what the British Army had learned about sniping had been worked out in the brutal years between 1915 and 1918. One of the greatest problems then was in finding the right men for the job, for there was an anomaly: good target shots selected for sniping duties often proved to be very bad snipers. They excelled on the ranges and could complete the arduous sniping training, but not every man had the mental strength to look into the face of a human target just before pulling the trigger. An artilleryman or machine gunner killed at a distance as their targets were often out of sight, or at least beyond a range where they were clearly identifiable as individual human beings. This placed a mental buffer-zone between the action of firing a weapon and the (often messy) end result. Uniquely among combat soldiers the snipers never had this luxury, hence Harry's distaste for seeing his first kill close-up.

It was a well-understood fact by 1939 that men required for sniping had to possess special qualities. Normally they were of a better-than-average educational standard, self-reliant, determined, but with a critical mental detachment that enabled them to kill without qualm. Hesketh-Prichard said, with much truth, that: 'Hunters, poachers and game-keepers' made the best snipers. In the formative years, the majority of snipers had been countrymen who understood the arts of stealth, stalking and patience, but by no means did that disqualify city dwellers from also becoming very competent and during 1915–18 they comprised the majority of sniper trainees. As a breed, Harry said:

> Snipers ... would not be the life and soul of a party as they were often quiet, unassuming and tended towards introspection.

But he clearly had what it took, being dispassionately professional. Indeed, he commented with some amusement that his regimental sergeant-major once told him that he 'had never come across a more unsociable NCO'. That he was so good at his trade is evidenced not only by the fact that he survived (he was the only Hallamshire regimental sniper who landed on D-Day to reach Germany), but that he unwittingly became Britain's highest scoring sniper. He realised that sniping would be the perfect solution to both his independent attitude and to the army's obsession with spit and polish. In this way, he found his ideal place within the military machine.

Chapter 2

Sniper Training and Equipment

BRITISH ARMY DOCTRINE IN 1941 dictated that eight snipers were to be allocated to every infantry battalion[1] and they were expected to work in pairs, one observing, the other waiting to take on a target. These roles were regularly reversed in order to provide their eyes with much-needed rest. Although this was the official requirement, there was always much latitude given as to how the snipers themselves wanted to work. Mostly, Harry did not like being with anyone else:

> In my own case I had a decided preference to work alone as it enabled me to get much closer to the enemy front-line areas, even at times going through them as well in order to observe their activities more clearly. As a bonus, it sometimes gave me the opportunity of sniping at very high priority targets, such as visiting senior officers who would seldom put themselves at risk by being in the forward positions.

Snipers' duties had much expanded from the Great War doctrine of 'dominate no-man's land', although it is to the credit of those involved that the early wartime training courses that had been developed proved over time to be both efficient and enduring. In many respects, much of what is still taught today in sniping schools rests on the shoulders of those early pioneers. In 1940, the manual printed for training was basically that of 1918 (albeit slightly updated) and when Harry was issued with his copy, he studied it intently, reading it over and over. He loved the discipline of accurate shooting: the breathing control, the arm and eye co-ordination, the steadiness of trigger pull, and, as he slowly began to appreciate, the manifold skills of learning to become invisible and to outwit his opponents in a game of hide-and-seek in which there was no second place. Shooting was obviously a vital part of his job but there was much, much more for a sniper to learn before he was let loose on the battlefield. The 'mission statement' as it would now be described, was quite straightforward and it still provides the foundation for modern sniper training.

- To anticipate enemy movement by observation properly related to intelligence.
- To deny enemy intelligence by sniping his observers, harassing his patrols and forestalling his raids.
- To establish a complete moral and physical domination of no-man's land if static warfare develops.

But to accomplish this, the list of what had to be learned by neophyte snipers was daunting. They had to master fieldcraft, map-reading, camouflage, observation and marksmanship, be capable of estimating distance and windspeed accurately (both extremely difficult skills to master), sketch clearly, write informative reports legibly, have the eyesight of a hawk and the patience of a cat. Harry's course began in late 1941 and lasted twelve weeks, broken into sections depending on what was to be taught. He was initially sent to one of the three sniper training centres: at Bisley Camp in Surrey, the School of Musketry in Hythe, and Llanberis in Snowdonia. Each centre performed a specific function, Bisley to qualify for shooting competence, Hythe to instruct in shooting theory and rifle care, and Llanberis for fieldcraft, camouflage and other external skills. Each part ended with a stiff examination and failure of any one part led to removal from the course. Indeed, the training was physically and mentally gruelling and the failure rate high. Almost 50 per cent of trainees were returned to their units as 'unsuitable for sniping'. Even today, second to Special Forces training, sniping has the highest failure rate of candidate specialists in the army. The point of sniping was not just to inflict physical damage on the enemy, it was also to lower his morale. When soldiers begin to notice that sudden killing shots were targeting officers, NCOs and other specialists, then they knew only too well that they were under observation from a sniper. Their unit morale might plummet and it could become almost impossible for officers to encourage men to obey orders in the face of such accurate fire. Usually, all available weaponry was brought in to counter this – mortars, medium machine guns, artillery. But most often the only practical response was to field their own snipers. As fighting in Normandy intensified in 1944, this frequently proved to be the only available solution, as opposing forces were so close to each other that shellfire was as dangerous to one side as the other. As Harry said, 'to catch a thief you need to send a thief in after him', and so the call for 'sniper forward' became commonplace. This resulted in an oddly ambivalent attitude among the British infantrymen, who on one hand understood the necessity of snipers clearing the way for them, but then did not really like the way that they did it. This was nothing new, for historically snipers had never comfortably rubbed shoulders with the ordinary soldier.

> It was quite a rigid ruling that snipers kept to themselves, and they were ordered not to discuss their role even with their mates in the rifle companies. This was to ensure that details of their operations, equipment in use, tactics etc., could not be revealed under interrogation by soldiers later captured ... for such information was always sought by each side as a matter of importance due to the constant losses of officers and senior NCOs to snipers. We had orders ... that the intelligence that we gathered in the course of sniper patrols was only to be discussed with our own senior officers and the Battalion 'I' [Intelligence] Section who quickly forwarded all useful information to rear HQ Intelligence.

During 1914–18, senior officers frequently exhibited open distaste for sniper units, some actually refusing to employ them. They were regarded with suspicion, as few understood what they did and many viewed them as no more than unprincipled killers. This attitude softened somewhat during the later years of WW1 as British snipers gained the upper hand and became far more appreciated for their intelligence-gathering skills. The WW2 instructors did not belabour the point officially, but Harry and his fellows spent much time talking to WWI veterans who pointed out the highly probable negative social consequences of their chosen profession.

> I recall[1] that our padre used to watch me going out on a patrol and would cheerfully call out 'The Grim Reaper is off again' though I regarded it in good part as front-line humour, and I had great respect for his personal bravery. It has to be admitted, though, that generally snipers are not popular soldiers in any army, and we were thought trouble-makers at times, for it is a strange fact that whilst front-line soldiers will accept shellfire, mortar barrages, air attacks and ... frequency of stray bullets flying around, they will all go in fear of a sniper. Nothing reduced a fighting man to uselessness quicker than seeing his officers or friends drop suddenly with the hallmark bullet through the head.

Having the equipment was all very well but it was then up to the instructors to ensure that their charges were trained to the highest possible levels when it came to using using it. Marksmanship, or, as one commented to Harry's class: 'putting round holes in square heads', was of paramount importance. All of the trainees were good shots, some being competitive target shooters, but there was a special art to combat shooting that had to be learned since, unlike on a range, a near-miss could cost the sniper his, or a comrade's life. Harry had learned all of the basics as a cadet, but was surprised to find how much more knowledge was required to become an effective sniper.

> We were taught about the proper method of holding the rifle, using the 1907 leather sling. This braced the left arm and when properly fitted enabled the rifle to sit in the shoulder and on the left palm, without the need to hold it with the right hand, and it should remain on target. Getting the sling exactly right was a fiddle but very necessary. We used the cheek-piece to obtain what was called a 'weld'. That was when the head was firmly in position, and we were looking through the scope. Initially, we were told not to use our right hand at all, and to place our hand on the ground. The target should remain clearly in sight, with the cross-

> hairs more or less perfectly in the centre. The right hand was then brought up to take up the first trigger pressure and to steady the rifle. We also had to learn to control our breathing, taking a breath then letting half go and holding it until we made the shot.

When regularly practised, this breathing control could also steady the sniper's heart rate and most could bring heart rate down at will after a few seconds, even after some exertion. It was vital because even a slightly thumping heart resulted in the fine crosshairs seeming to leap around the target of their own volition. The trigger of each rifle had been carefully prepared by the gunsmith who assembled it[2] to be both smooth and consistent (the factory triggers were often very heavy). Each trigger had two positions, a slightly slack first, then a firmer second.

> A pressure of around five pounds would fire the shot and our instructor drummed into us that we must *always* squeeze the trigger, never pull it. I had been instructed to do this as a cadet, for on the ranges I had learned that even a very slightly clumsy trigger pull would render the shot inaccurate.

Only constant range practice, in every type of weather, could provide the men with the experience they needed and each course at sniper school specialised in differing elements of training. The Small Arms School Sniping Wing at Bisley in Surrey developed a specialised course for care and use of the No. 32 scope and the 22× Scout Regiment telescope. It also taught the snipers in great detail the complex methods of telescopic-sight adjustment, estimating range and wind strength. They were also inculcated into the grisly, but necessary, vital points of aim on the human body.

> We were always taught well to deliver our shots to maximum effect, so we went for head shots to eliminate instantly from battle those we targeted. The ideal point of aim for this was the mouth, for it allowed a little leeway if range had been under or over-estimated; shoot high, and you hit the forehead, low and the throat or chest, all were killing shots. Snipers were *not trained to wound* and a well-

placed head shot would result in instant death. In combat we found this to be vital and in one instance one of our snipers shot a Waffen-SS soldier through the heart and he continued to advance, firing his Schmeisser sub-machine gun before he fell dead. Up to 300 yards we went for head-shots, 400 yards and over we went for point of impact on the body mass, particularly if they were moving.

The School of Musketry at Hythe specialised in long-range shooting, building on the initial shooting instruction at Bisley and teaching the snipers exactly how difficult it was to place shots accurately at 600 yards and beyond.

> We were all quite competent, at least we thought so, but shooting at these long ranges was a whole new world to us. A very few of the men had done this at Bisley, but combat shooting was very different and learning to calculate *exactly* the range and wind to within a few yards or miles an hour was difficult. I would at times shoot up to 1,000 yards, but for that sort of long-range shooting I had many calculations to make very quickly in order to ensure my bullet hit my point of aim. We had a preference to use our range and deflection drums rather than use 'Kentucky windage'[3] guesswork. Sometimes there was no time for using our scope drums, however, and we made allowance by eye. On occasions when the enemy counter-attacked, we became exceptionally active and often we would pick off enemy soldiers getting into better positions. We particularly targeted machine gunners, portable flame-throwers, anti-tank gunners, mortar crews and any officers or NCOs. We ... were often responsible for inflicting heavy losses on the enemy.

The instructors were a mixed bunch, with some regular officers and NCOs, many of whom had learned their trade in the trenches of Flanders in the previous war. Some had been professional big-game hunters and others very successful long-range target shooters; all of them, Harry said, were 'at the top of their game'.

> Thinking back to those earlier times I have had many regrets that I didn't keep a note of the names of the mature civilian

marksmen who volunteered to come and pass on expertise, all of them were outstanding Bisley 'Gravelbellies'.[4] We had, of course, very efficient instructors from the Small Arms School, but it was the more mature distinguished crack-shots who had been so well-known pre-WW2, who came in and patiently taught us the best techniques. It was from them that I first learned of what was known as Khyber Factor, that curious phenomenon of high-angle shooting, uphill or downhill, when you make a minimum allowance and aim lower. It seems they had first known of the Khyber Factor from the nineteenth-century experiences of our Martini-armed riflemen fighting in the Afghan Wars, often fought on the steep inclines of the Khyber Pass. I believe this is now known as 'high and low incline shooting'.

Naturally, the training was not purely weapons-based, for the army had long realised that snipers were unrivalled in their ability to observe and note down enemy troop movements, locations of armour, artillery and mortar units, and even determine what regiments were dug-in in front of them. This was in part due to their unique use of the 22× Scout Telescope, a powerful optical tool that no other army ever adopted. Used for decades by the Scottish ghillies[5] in the Highlands for deer-stalking, a good glassman[6] with his telescope was able to see a deer at five miles in clear weather, and at closer ranges the telescope often enabled a sniper or his observer to determine what insignia a German was wearing, see unit markings on vehicles or find heavily camouflaged positions. The days of spotting a potential target and simply shooting at it were long gone, and much of the sniper's work involved lying patiently and invisibly in a hide for hours on end, making notes and drawings of what was observed. They were lectured at some length in the technicalities of intelligence-gathering, for it was understood by the outbreak of war that shooting individual enemy soldiers rarely had any effect on the eventual outcome of a battle, but good intelligence could, and as a result the sniper sections became very highly valued for this skill which was to become their most important battlefield function. Harry frequently commented that it was considered more vital to report on enemy movements and strength than shoot anyone. Every sniper always carried a simple notebook in which were recorded:

> ... any relevant details we observed on our patrols, such as shots fired and possible results, times of such incidents, recognition of enemy units from uniform insignia, enemy movements, heavy weapons, any type of tracked or wheeled transport, results of our shelling or mortar fire. Map references had to be given for each item noted. Plus, anything else we saw that might be of possible use to our own battalion 'I' officer.

When Harry's course moved to the Army School of Fieldcraft and Sniping at Llanberis in Snowdonia, the school was under the command of Major J. Wills, an ex-WW1 Lovat Scout and a highly respected officer. The second-in-command at Llanberis, Major Underhill, was also something of a hero to Harry, having served under Hesketh-Prichard at the First Army Sniping School during the First World War. He gave Harry his personally inscribed copy of the *Manual of Map Reading and Field Sketching*, with its official stamp 'First Army School of Scouting Observation and Sniping. Do Not Take Away, Course Use Only.'

Former Lovat Scouts like Major Wills were an elite group of men whose skills proved fundamental to the effective training of the British snipers in both world wars. The Lovats were formed in 1899 during the Second Boer War and recruited Highland ghillies, who, it soon became clear, had unparalleled abilities to stalk and observe enemy forces. They thus became the army's unofficial intelligence-gatherers. After the Boer War the Lovats survived as a Territorial unit and in WW1 they initially formed the first sniping units on the Western Front. Their numbers were too small to be effective, however, and the authorities decided that their skills would be far better put to use instructing the hundreds of snipers starting to pass through the various sniping schools that were being set up. The Lovats remained in this role throughout WW2, but some also fought as a combat battalion in Italy, specialising in mountain warfare.

Harry was slightly in awe of them:

I have always had the greatest respect for the Lovat Scouts, they are unique, elite and they have truly earned their place in sniper history. During my training, I had already gone through two earlier sniper courses for specialists at Bisley and Hythe under mainly WW1-era instructors, both soldiers and also a couple of mature civilians who were big-game hunters who had taught us advanced riflecraft. But it was at Llanberis ... that I had my main contact with the famous Lovat Scouts. Our Camp Commandant was a Scout and with him were some Lovat Scout sergeant-instructors who were the finest 'glassmen' I had ever encountered, for their abilities with the 22× (telescope) were breath-taking in the minute detail they could uncover. Moreover, their skills in silent stalking combined with [use of] natural camouflage proved them masters of getting into positions unobserved. We learned so much from them that I am quite sure they gave us the 'edge' when we went into action later. Every sniper who came under their instruction is indebted to them as supreme experts in fieldcraft. Mind you, I do recall that all of us Sassenachs had a minor problem deciphering

How camouflage should work. An image of an apparently empty field with a bush in it – one of a series of taken for training purposes and used in lectures.

their heavy Highland brogue, but they easily got over that by clearly demonstrating their methods better than any spoken word.

This of course implied that the sniper could actually get to the position he had selected without being observed and a lot of practice was devoted to ensuring that they remained invisible to an experienced and observant enemy.

At sniping school, we were taught to move from a start line 1,000 yards distant to our allocated position which would perhaps be only 100 yards from the school instructors, and then fire a blank round, all to be unobserved by them. At times it would take us a few hours to travel a short distance; we very quietly and very slowly crawled at a snail's pace with long waits every few yards to get where we needed to go.

It was utterly exhausting work made all the more difficult because the very experienced instructors used their Scout Telescopes to spot for movement and knew, almost to the yard, from which

The three snipers who were hidden in the previous photograph. When properly camouflaged they were expected to be invisible at five paces.

direction the snipers were coming. Snipers learned how to crawl while balancing the heavy rifle on one or both out-stretched arms, making use of every dip and furrow and lying as still as statues if they believed they might be under observation. Movement was the most frequent give-away leading to discovery and death for inexperienced snipers. The teaching of outdoor navigation skills was a major part of the syllabus as accurately pinpointing positions on a map left no room for errors. If artillery or mortar fire was to be called upon to strike enemy positions, even the slightest error in the co-ordinates given could result in the target either being missed, giving the Germans a chance to escape, or worse leading to Allied forward units being hit. Harry also remarked that every intelligence report had to be started afresh every day and written in block capitals so no report could be misread by anyone; this was a habit that he was to continue for the rest of his life when leaving a message. Deciphering a map correctly was not as easy as it first appeared and such work required considerable proficiency, not only in map-reading but in compass work – skills not everyone was able to master. In particular the use of the prismatic compass was considered vital and was taught as part of early basic training, to allow a sniper to provide precise degree bearings that could be cross-checked against a map. This was practised over and over in the field, as at times plotting a compass bearing was often the only available method for a sniper or patrol to find their way back to their own lines. This was particularly true in heavily wooded country, or if fog or darkness had descended.

> On several occasions, I was glad that I had taken bearings from my start point, as it was so easy in wooded country to become hopelessly lost, more so in poor light or at night. Even so, on one or two occasions I decided to stop and take cover until it became lighter, as I was not convinced I was heading in the correct direction, and many a rifle patrol has blundered into enemy lines after becoming disorientated in bad weather or darkness.

Maps were not the only method of pinpointing enemy units, however, and the increasing use of aerial reconnaissance by both sides meant that snipers had to be taught the basics of deciphering reconnaissance photographs of the surrounding landscape. Of course, they did not need to reach the proficiency of the professional photo-analysts in their intelligence sections, but being able to match personal observations to a photographic image of something spotted deep behind enemy lines was at times extremely useful.

> Occasionally, I would report perhaps that there was heavy dust from vehicles, two miles or more away from my position but of course it was beyond my ability to determine what [it was]. Using a map meant that I could more-or-less pinpoint a crossroads or something similar but when I returned to 'I' they often produced very high quality photographs of the ground behind the German lines, and we could compare my sightings and see that there was what might be a tank laager[7] or mortar pit under camouflage. Then they would call artillery or an aircraft attack on it. If you asked a brigade Intelligence officer what he considered of prime importance, a high body count from snipers or highly detailed military intelligence, he would undoubtedly tell you that first and foremost he wanted information.

Sometimes snipers provided the only way of determining if the Germans were trying out a deception or were genuinely planning an offensive move. One example Harry recalled was when a forward British position reported hearing tracked vehicles being moved up at night, which could be the precursor to an attack by tanks or self-propelled (SP) guns. This would mean having to move an anti-tank unit forward, always with the risk of discovery and with considerable physical effort in the *bocage* country of Normandy.

> After dusk, two of our snipers were sent out beyond our lines and they returned to report that they had seen a heavyweight truck fitted with a loudspeaker!

The weeks of tough training equipped the snipers with the skills they required to become effective and survive. The final part was undertaken in the wilds of Snowdonia. This, Harry recalled, was done in his case in appalling weather conditions, very cold with driving rain and sleet, but he said that he enjoyed it immensely!

Everything we had learned was thrown at us at Llanberis, we had to reach our targets unseen, place shots accurately, find hidden targets then use maps and compass bearings to report their positions precisely, any errors made lost one marks.

It was made all the more difficult because of the weather, but as our instructors said, the weather will throw everything at you when you are in the lines and we'd better get used to it. One problem we all had was that our scopes misted up due to the rain and on the early scopes it was hard to prevent this. The later Mk III [scopes] were waterproofed, but we didn't have them and misting was a constant problem as moisture got into the body of the scope and fogged the lenses. These couldn't be dried off like the exterior of the lenses, and could render the scope useless. So, we went to great lengths to keep them dry. We would keep the rifles tucked inside our smocks, often wrapped in a waterproof sheet. In extreme cold weather the warmth of our faces instantly misted up the ocular[8] lens so we sometimes dismounted them (the scopes) which we hated doing and put them inside our clothing, mounting them only when it was necessary.

Although tough, the training in Snowdonia proved priceless for it provided the nearest experience that the snipers could get to actual combat. One practice routine was to prove of particular importance following D-Day, and that was to locate and eliminate an 'enemy' sniper. The 'enemy' was an instructor in full camouflage carefully concealed under the watchful gaze of another instructor. The time taken by an approaching trainee sniper to find and deal with him successfully by firing a blank round was then recorded. Of course, the trainee sniper should not, at any time, be spotted. This was undertaken in every conceivable weather condition and terrain, which made it all the more difficult.

Hunting another sniper was always a tense operation and fraught with difficulties. Open country was the most challenging, as there was such a limited number of places to hide, whereas urban sniping held limitless possibilities of cover ... and sometimes we watched for hours through the telescope, taking it in turns so as to rest our eyes. When we spotted, or thought we had, the hidden man, we made very careful notes including compass bearings and fired a blank shot. That signalled to the instructors that we had succeeded. Little did we know how close to reality it would be once we had landed in Normandy. The *bocage* was particularly difficult and there was nothing very similar in England that compared with it.

None of this was yet known to Harry who graduated as a sniper in late 1943 and then embarked on more months of training in England – much of it in the West Country – without any knowledge of what they were training for, or where they would be going.

We knew that it involved a sea crossing, as we did some training on assault landing craft on the south-west coast, which was quite interesting, but a lot of it was village fighting and we had use of some small villages that had been cleared of their inhabitants. I recall one was Tyneham, which I'm sure was once very pretty, but the army had made quite a mess of it. I suppose it was vital to our training, but we often wondered what would become of the inhabitants after the war. We learned about street fighting and how we snipers could be most effectively employed. This was by providing cover for our own infantry by concealing ourselves in roof spaces with a good view of the buildings and ground ahead, or moving up with them to deal with any sudden targets, such as machine guns.

The Enfield No. 4 (T) Rifle and No. 32 Telescopic Sight

The development of the Enfield No. 4 (T) sniping rifle and its No. 32 telescopic sight is covered in more detail in Appendix 1 of this book, but an overview of the weapon that served Harry so well is important at this point to understand how vital it was in bringing out the very best of the sniper's capabilities. The old Lee-Enfield Mk III of pre-Great War vintage was a beautifully manufactured weapon, made to exacting peacetime standards, but by the mid-

1920s it was clearly near the end of its lifespan. Post-war it was too slow and costly to manufacture and from its introduction it had suffered from a number of minor but irritating shortcomings. Whilst its basic design as a combat rifle was very sound, it needed updating, and some deficiencies required remedying. In particular it provided a poor view through its iron sights because the distance between the front and rear sights was too short, and the all-enclosing barrel woodwork adversely affected accuracy once wet. So, after considerable testing and troop-trialling in the 1930s, the final incarnation was introduced into army service in late 1941. This was the Rifle No. 4 Mk 1 .303 inch, which addressed the problems of the earlier model as well as incorporating several improvements.

The most immediately visible change was the loss of the distinctive snub-nosed projecting bayonet lug at the muzzle, which instead had a protruding muzzle, as well as a much-improved design of rear sight, with a small peep-sight for battle ranges. Other changes, which are looked at in more detail in Appendix 1, were introduced to speed up production. While this was fine for what was to be a mass-produced combat rifle, what the manufacturing plants at Maltby, Fazakerley and Birmingham could not undertake was the time-consuming precision work required to turn one into a very accurate sniping rifle. As experience had shown in the previous war, an off-the-production-line rifle with a scope bolted on was simply not good enough for the long ranges at which the snipers expected to fight. Accuracy was paramount for snipers.

However, there was a problem with the availability of the No. 4 rifles for training; they were in very short supply and the sniping variant was completely unobtainable. So Harry was initially issued with a World War One Pattern 1914, Mk I (T) Enfield rifle and Aldis Pattern 1918 telescopic sight. These all came from existing stores and were set up by Alex Martin of Glasgow. It was actually a very effective pairing, and many hundreds were hurriedly assembled from stores in 1939 as a stopgap measure until a proper sniping rifle could be produced. Many early snipers actually regarded the P. 14 rifle as superior to the No. 4, in part because it had excellent micro-adjustable iron sights, which greatly aided accurate shooting at most ranges. Harry liked it very much, believing it had a far better trigger action and superior accuracy to the SMLEs, and he used one for all of his early training. Fortunately for the snipers, supplies of the purpose-built No. 4 (T) rifle began to appear in 1942, many of these being converted from early 1930's No. 4 trials rifles that had been field-tested by armourers and instructors. As production increased, these long-awaited weapons began to arrive in quantity and trainee snipers were soon each issued with what the army termed a Complete Equipment Schedule or 'CES'. It was, as Harry said 'like Christmas', when the wooden transit chests arrived and were signed for by every sniper. Each one contained everything

An almost 'Complete Equipment Schedule', as replicated for himself by a former Normandy sniper and fellow target shooter the author knew in the 1990s. It comprises a transit chest for the No. 4 (T) rifle and from top left: the metal carry-case and No. 32 Mk II telescopic sight; a long Bren gun webbing sling; Scout Regiment telescope and case; 1944-dated No. 4 (T) rifle with M. 1907 leather sling; a pair of Parker-Hale two-piece cleaning rods; a cigarette tin with a couple of .303 ammunition clips, two spare Mills grenade pins, some spare mounting screws for the telescope and mount; a No. 36 Mills grenade; prismatic compass; and Fairbairn-Sykes knife.
The issue 6×30 binoculars are missing.

required, at least, as far as the army was concerned: an Enfield No. 4 (T) rifle with its paired No. 32 telescope, American-supplied Pattern 1907 double-loop leather rifle sling, a pair of British-issue 6×30 binoculars and their leather or webbing carry-case, a Scout Regiment Mk II telescope and leather carry-case, rifle cleaning kit, luminous General Service pocket watch (American-manufactured, usually by Elgin)[9] a prismatic compass, a camouflage face veil, and a webbing carry-case for the rifle. A small tin of spare parts was included but a vital item not present at the time was the Fairbairn-Sykes fighting knife. Originally designed for the Commandos, its qualities soon became legendary and before D-Day snipers were each issued with one. Harry was never without his. Although he never used his for fighting – 'I never stabbed any gentlemen wearing grey-green uniforms' – they were employed in probing for mines and for more mundane jobs such as opening tins, venting the self-heating food rations,[10] and cutting up camouflage fabric.

> It was issued to me either late in 1943 or perhaps early 1944 and I wore it strapped to my right leg as I waded ashore on the Normandy landings. My original Fairbairn-Sykes leather scabbard did not hold the blade securely. In an attack on German positions, I noticed I'd lost my blade, it was only later as we secured the position, I made time to go back over the route I'd taken and luckily there it was, sticking point down in the ground. Not long afterwards I did a swap with an American paratrooper for his plastic-like scabbard which held his fighting knife inside a clip (I think I gave him an Iron Cross). I didn't want his knife, just the scabbard that held my blade securely.

Very oddly, the No. 4 Mk I spike bayonet (the so-called 'pig-sticker') was also issued, but hardly ever carried by snipers. Harry was quite damming on the subject of these anachronistic items.

> Whilst bayonets were issued to snipers they were *never, ever mounted on the rifle, never, as they destroy the zero of that precision rifle*. Bayonets are never a part of the equipment normally issued to snipers, so they were only ever used to prod for mines.

A two-piece cleaning rod, different to the standard pull-through, issued to the infantry was also included, as Harry explained:

> The chest had a ... rifle rod not pull-through which over time, we were told, caused barrel damage. In particular it could wear the muzzle unevenly which affected the bullet as it left the barrel. The brass weight on it was not a good idea either, although for the infantry, who mostly shot at close ranges, these factors were, I suppose, of little consequence. We were delighted when some No. 4 (T) rifles arrived in chests; we had not had a chance to handle one with its telescopic sight before and there was a great deal of interest in them. Our instructors at once began to use them and the old Enfields were quickly relegated to a store. We expected them to be rather well used, but it appeared that all had been sent to Holland & Holland[11] for refurbishment before coming to us.

Harry also had an interesting insight into the manufacture of some of the very rare Savage No. 4 (T) rifles issued. Almost 1.2 million of these were manufactured in the USA during the war, but it has long been held that none were ever converted for sniping. This was not the case, according to Harry:

> To keep costs down, the British Ministry of Supply ordered a very large consignment of No. 4 Lee-Enfield rifles from Savage. But the order was for a much lower specification having only two-groove barrels etc. ... intended only for support troops (RASC, RAOC, Signals, artillery etc., but not infantry). Savage have always been top-class manufacturers, so were a bit miffed not to get an order for high-spec rifles too ... so without direct orders they made a batch of truly high-spec No. 4 rifles with five- or six-groove barrels, selected black walnut stocks etc. ... a very, very few ended up as 4 (T) models and were fitted with Mk II telescopic sights made in Leeds. Mine was one of these specials. It was recognised that the Mk II scope was to all intents and purposes made regardless of cost, so in spite of the later upgraded Mk III, almost all of us had a preference for the Mk II which was so ruggedly built.

As undoubtedly one of the most crucial factors for a successful sniping rifle is its long-range capability, there was initially a question as to what sort of suitable telescope sight could be used. As experienced shooters say, 'If you can't see it, you can't hit it.' In fairness this had been recognised as a problem by the army a decade previously, and it was a coincidental but fortunate accident that a suitable optical sight was already in existence, having been designed in 1935 for fitting to the Bren light machine gun. This, and no pun intended, was a far-sighted move on behalf of the Royal Small Arms Factory (RSAF) Enfield, as it would have been the first ever British automatic weapon to be fitted with an optical sight. But it was never to be, for the exigencies of a wartime economy meant that the prototype scopes were left languishing in stores. Someone at the factory clearly realised that with some small design modifications, it would make a very effective sniping scope and at 3×, it was just about sufficient for long-range shooting; although greater magnification would have been an asset, the practicalities of obtaining different lenses and altering the technical specifications proved too great, given the required timescale. If the magnification itself was not as great as the snipers would have liked, the telescopes themselves were far tougher and more sophisticated than anything seen in the previous war. The reticles (or cross-hairs) followed the normal military pattern of having a vertical pointer nicknamed a 'fence-post' with a pointed tip and a fine horizontal cross-hair. The disadvantage of using this pattern rather than the usual commercial pair of fine cross-hairs was that at extreme range, the post could obscure the target, as a man at 800 yards is a very small target indeed. Helpfully, the scopes had a much broader field of view than the telescopes of a generation before. It was a little over 8 degrees, which made following a moving target considerably easier. More practically, there were now built-in range and elevation drums which had a click-stop adjustment. The range drum incorporated trajectory compensation, allowing for the falling curve of the bullet as range increased and the deflection (windage) drum enabled the sniper to calculate lateral bullet drift, depending on wind strength. These were fine skills that were honed with experience.

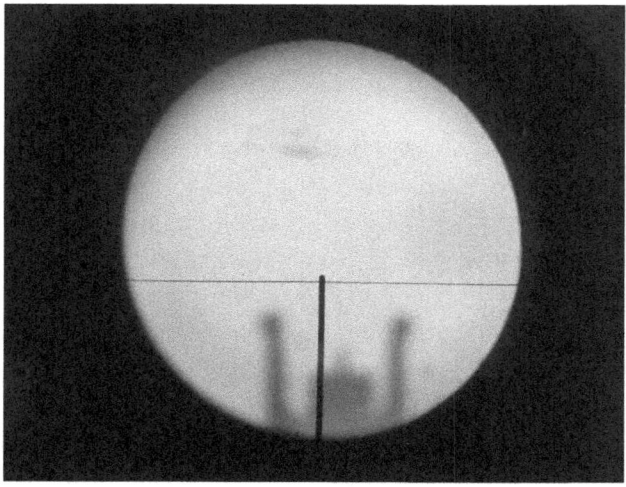

The view through Harry's No. 32 Mk II telescopic sight, showing the vertical post and crosshairs. Due to the lens configuration of the camera the blurred outline of the foresight is just visible, but would not be seen by the sniper.

To guess with some certainty the range and the wind force, which could be coming at a tangent or be a direct crosswind, became an art form in itself. A bullet fired will rise then fall in its trajectory on its way to the target, and the precise bullet drop needs to be known to hit the target exactly where you want the bullet to strike. In the same way the force of any wind during the bullet's flight will greatly affect the accuracy placement. Estimating distance on the flat is not too difficult with experience, but estimating distance which is uphill or downhill or across ravines or valleys can be very misleading.

I should give a few details about the difference in the Marks of our telescopic sight … we generally worked with the Mark II which I got to know very well indeed and could adjust in darkness to the precise adjustment I knew I'd need. The Mark II could be adjusted more precisely than the Mark I, but still needed special tools to re-zero, if they were available. The Mark III was much easier to re-zero and you could do it with the point of a .303 ball round, instead of a tool.

The many references Harry makes to accuracy must be understood in the context of the nature of wartime sniping, as he explains:

> Unlike shooting on a competitive rifle range when sighting and warm-up shots were on occasion allowable, in action under battle conditions we all had to make that first shot count, for there were no second chances. Amongst ourselves, rather than talk in range calculations as being in so many hundreds of yards, we used to talk in 'clicks' for the range and deflection drums. In the sniper's light[12] semi-dark of dawn and dusk and in particular when we were in a hide in which the interior was kept dark, it was essential that we could operate our telescopic sights quickly and click into position the range to our selected target, and then make the essential allowance for wind drift.

The very delicate adjustment on the scopes did have an inherent problem whereby the graticules would not always settle into the correct position when the drums were turned. There was a simple solution, however.

> It was always best to give to give additional clicks *over* estimated range and then immediately bring the drum down in clicks to the exact range I wanted. The reason was that wear and tear within the graticule movement of the centre-post and fine cross-wire meant that at times the internal mechanism did not go into position first time, so produced a sort of minor backlash movement. For example, if I wanted to shoot ... at 550 yards, then I would click my drum to 650 yards first, then immediately reverse my clicks to come back down onto 550 yards. This was not necessary when the scopes were new but in action as the TS [telescopic sight] took on more and more wear it was found to be the better way to stop the backlash effect.

Another problem that the sniper found when shooting any quantity of ammunition that the recoil of the rifle loosened screws.

> Before any shooting, we all made a point of double-checking the rigidity of our telescopic sights, so all screws

were checked for tightness, particularly the front lug-pad screws holding the TS bracket as these could loosen with the continual heavy recoil. Later the REME[13] armourers found that spiking the screws in position with a centre-punch meant they would not move.

The requirement for a precise first-shot placement was simple; the German snipers were highly professional and would retaliate in seconds if a shot missed its intended target. Rifles also needed re-zeroing if the scope was regularly removed, different ammunition types were used, or if accidental mishandling had knocked it. If the zero was not absolutely precise, a shot might only miss by inches: but that could seal the sniper's fate. Depending on circumstances, a sniper rarely fired any more than two shots, and normally evacuated his position as fast and stealthily as possibly as soon as he had. Harry said he would sometimes fire two, and on extremely rare occasions three shots, depending on how well concealed he was.

> We had to re-zero our rifles when it was needed ... in action rifles and sights take a lot of harsh treatment, so it becomes necessary quite often to re-check the scope for point-of-aim accuracy, for precise shooting is the hallmark of any sniper. Whenever we had a fault with a particular rifle or telescopic sight, they both had to be sent back together to a mobile REME armourers' workshop for adjustment and repair. Each telescopic sight was especially finely adjusted to fit a particular rifle, and could not be interchanged with any other sniping rifle. I should mention that a sniper's rifle and telescopic sight can only be adjusted for correct zero *to one man only*. It is not transferable to another sniper if extreme accuracy is to be retained. Obviously at times with a two-man team the same rifle might on occasion be shared, but even that was never advisable ... the variance in eyesight, breath control, exact position of head and cheek rest whilst firing, trigger sensitivity etc. are all essential aspects which must be tuned in to a specific rifle.

Any serious mechanical problem resulted in the sniper being without his rifle, and Harry heartily disliked such a situation, so decided to solve the problem in his own unique way, by unofficially acquiring a 'No. 2, No. 4' rifle![14] He did not smoke so was able to use his cigarette ration to bribe (he preferred to say 'persuade') the unit armourers to indent for another No. 4 (T) rifle which was duly handed over to him, and he used both throughout the campaign. It will re-surface later on in his story.

There was another, oft-overlooked aspect to rifle ownership and that was the dull but vitally important process of keeping it clean and functioning efficiently. For the ordinary riflemen of the infantry companies, the cleanliness of their weapons was a matter to be dealt with as and when circumstances permitted. If one of their rifles failed to function, obtaining another was seldom a problem and machine guns had working parts that were easily changed, leaving dirty or broken components to be cleaned or discarded depending on the circumstances. To achieve the required cleanliness Harry said 'it was drummed into us like a mantra' to be obsessive about the condition of their rifles, scopes, and their ammunition. Sniping rifles were in a different league to infantry rifles, being high-precision weapons and the snipers relied utterly on their accuracy being consistent:

> ... on the premise that if you don't look after your rifle, it might fail you when the chips are down in battle. No matter how exhausted I was on returning to our lines after a sniper patrol, I insisted that nobody else cleaned my No. 4 (T). I had bought my own Parker-Hale take-down cleaning rod set and also a supply of cleaning chemicals, but I used to boil water in my mess-tin over a petrol and sand fire when back at HQ to clean the bore properly.[15]

The issue of cleaning was not just one of ensuring the efficient working of the rifle but also one of accuracy. The quality of steel used for the barrels was nowhere near as good as in today's rifles, and the service life of a No. 4 (T) was estimated to be no more than 1,000 rounds before accuracy began to drop off. Harry commented that use of special-purpose ammunition, which is covered in the following section, could often reduce this to 500 rounds. This then required the rifle to be returned to the unit armourers who could replace the barrel, as a small stock of selected replacements was held. However, once returned, the sniper had to ensure it met his required standard of accuracy which was a time-consuming task as it had to be carefully re-zeroed. Any really badly damaged or non-functioning rifles would be returned to Holland & Holland for refurbishment, necessitating the issue of a new rifle to the sniper.

One factor that all snipers were aware of, and the reason why Harry used a commercial cleaning-rod set, was the inadequacy of the issue pull-through supplied with the standard infantry rifles. This was of heavy cord with loops at one end and a metal weight at the other. When dropped into the chamber with an oiled piece of flannelette in the loop (the ubiquitous 'four by two') it was pulled through from the muzzle end to clean the bore. Harry and most of his fellow snipers disliked them.

Although snipers are obviously defined by their unique scoped rifles, they were often required to carry secondary arms for close self-defence. After D-Day Harry was, much to his disgust, issued with a silenced Sten sub-machine gun.

> I said I was a trained sniper, not an ordinary infantryman, but I was issued with a silenced Sten gun as a getaway weapon if cornered. I didn't like being bogged down with too much to carry when I had to move silently most of the time. When I tried it out, I found that it had been previously damaged by someone trying it out in fully-automatic mode.[16] They ruined all the internal baffles in the silencer. Some snipers did carry a sound-moderated Sten but I soon stopped carrying mine.

He did, however, carry a .38-calibre revolver in a web holster on his belt as a last-ditch sidearm. It should be said that some snipers in close-combat zones such as towns did find a Sten or a captured German MP 40 sub-machine gun useful, but a sniper much preferred to do what he was trained to do, which was the accurate targeting of enemy soldiers. As Harry once dryly commented, if a sniper found himself in close combat like that, something had gone very wrong! Useful pieces of weaponry that all snipers carried in the cavernous pockets of their Denison smocks were two No. 36

Mills grenades. They were seldom used in anger but were helpful in providing a diversion if required, or to clear suspect buildings or slit trenches that were considered too dangerous to approach. Generally, snipers preferred to work with infantry in urban situations and leave grenade and close-combat work to them, but this was not always possible.

Ammunition

So often overlooked, the quality of ammunition used was utterly fundamental to the success of a sniper, as it determined the precision of his shooting. On the face of it, it seems unnecessary to dwell on the technicalities of a cartridge for it is merely a receptacle that holds the powder charge, enabling the bullet to be fired. But, as is usual with anything technical, the reality is a much more complex subject than it first appears. This is not the place for a treatise on ballistics, but Harry made constant references to ammunition in his writing and there was good reason for this. No matter how brilliant the sniper was, or how precisely zeroed his rifle, if his ammunition did not perform faultlessly, and consistently, he might as well not bother shooting. The last thing any soldier wanted was a rifle that jammed in combat and for a sniper it meant that a particularly vital shot could be missed and he could expect retaliation. Poor cartridges with visible corrosion, dented brass, badly inserted primers or improperly seated bullets would adversely affect accuracy, or simply fail to ignite. Resultantly, the snipers took very particular care of their ammunition, often to the bemusement of their infantry rifle companies, who could not understand the apparent obsession the sniper sections had with examining and cleaning their cartridges. There was, of course, sound reasoning to this:

> We cleaned our ammo, as dirty cases affect the smoothness of loading and can affect the head-space[17] in the receiver and that leads to trouble – jamming at times or wild shots. In the same way we had to keep our ammo dry in the magazines, for wet rounds are bad news for snipers. If it was raining and we needed to reload, the general technique was to tip the rifle to the right towards the ground, and then cycle the bolt upside down, to keep the rain out. If it

was drenching rain, we would slide the rifles underneath our bodies to keep the magazines dry.

Among other problems, water on ammunition can raise chamber pressures when the rifle is fired, leading to inaccuracy. The backward thrust of the bolt on firing is increased as the expanding case cannot compress the water droplets. This in turn leads to excessive barrel jump and range tests showed this can alter the impact point of a bullet by up to 7 inches at 100 yards. It can also result in damaged primers, leaving tiny pieces of metal in the chamber that prevent another round being fed in.

> Unfortunately, the standard .303-inch service rounds did not provide extreme-range accuracy, whilst giving excellent service for the use of the rifle companies who rarely had to do any extreme-range shooting. The tasks of a sniper are quite different and he is expected to be able to eliminate enemy soldiers by firing just one shot at all ranges up to many hundreds of yards… every time. At sniping school, we were promised that rear supplies would send the sniping sections special batches of tested ammunition of a Match Standard[18] suitable for competitive shooting for instance. In practice this did not happen … and it was very important to try and find ammo from the best makers. It was a job to do so and we favoured Winchester, or sometimes a specific batch of British-made cartridges that proved especially good. Later on, I discovered that our support medium machine gunners (Vickers machine gun), the 2nd Battalion Kensingtons, occasionally got special long-range .303 supplies for specific shoots, then I used to go over to their slit trenches and offer my cigarette rations in exchange for a batch I could use. The Kensingtons thought it was a scream I should be cadging their ammo, but I found it no hardship as I was a non-smoker anyway. The cartridges were in boxes marked 'MK VIIIz'.[19] As supplies were not plentiful, I could only get small batches at a time. My visits … were even mentioned when the 2nd Kensingtons held a re-union in London post-war, so it seems my cadging visits struck a chord!

In terms of special-purpose ammunition, there were very few options available to the snipers during the war. Aside from the heavier long-range Mk VIIIz machine-gun ammunition, there were:

> ... three main types of ammunition. Normal high-velocity rounds, which we cleaned carefully before use to ensure correct chambering, and to make sure they never went into the chamber wet. In addition, we carried armour-piercing ammunition and incendiary rounds. We were supposed to carry tracer as well, but very few snipers ever did so. Use of tracer would immediately give away our position, though very occasionally we would fire it towards concealed targets to help an artillery FOO (Forward Observation Officer). When we went into action, we carried a few mags pre-loaded with five rounds, one with ordinary ball, one with AP and one with incendiary but *never ever* tracer. Also to be taken into consideration was the fact that tracer, AP or Incendiary are the cause of excessive wear ... and over-use of such ammunition drastically shortens the life of the barrel. Whenever possible, we kept a note of how many rounds we fired to determine how much life the barrel had left in it. We never carried a lot of ammunition; we always used to say any sniper who went out with too much ammunition, wouldn't return.

Although the snipers were issued with the standard 50-round cloth ammunition bandoliers, naturally they did things differently.

> I *never* used the cloth bandoliers, we used to take all the ammunition out of their five-round clips, as in any case we could not load charger-load our rifles with the telescopic sight in place. Then we would clean all the cartridges and carry them loose.

There has been much debate post-war about the use of explosive ammunition by snipers and Harry had this to say on the matter:

> Never, ever did we come across an example of such ammunition being used in combat. For a start it wasn't very

accurate and there was simply no point to it being used. Both sides needed extreme accuracy, not the devastating effects of explosive bullets, which were actually produced for aerial use. We used incendiary occasionally to set fire to something like a haystack that we suspected of harbouring a sniper, but it was very rare. After the war, I read of stories of the German and Russian snipers using explosive bullets on each other, but I really cannot see the point. I think there was a lot of confusion caused among infantrymen by the awful nature of the wounds inflicted by ordinary high-velocity bullets. At close range they would shatter major bones and they created large exit wounds that looked to the inexperienced like the result of explosive rounds. The same happened during the 1914–18 war when it was commonly believed each side used explosive or Dum Dum bullets.[20]

There was also an unresolved question about the use by Germans of sound-suppressed rifles with sub-sonic ammunition. Harry did not, in all his combat time, see evidence of any rifles being fitted with sound suppressors and it is unproven if any were provided to snipers. There were a number of technical reasons for this. Aside from the high cost of manufacture, a suppressor cannot be used with high-velocity ammunition, as it could not mask the distinctive 'crack' of the supersonic bullet. In addition, the pressure generated would simply blow the suppressor's silencing baffles apart. What he did come across, however, was sub-sonic ammunition that fired a bullet at below the speed of sound (1,125 fps) and this could be used in an ordinary rifle and considerably muted the sound of the shot.

> We did think it likely that the German had indeed made use of sub-sonic ammunition at times, for [it] makes it hard to locate the position it was fired from. Later we heard a German truck was found loaded with ammunition marked *Unterschall* ('sub-sonic') but it was snatched by our IO so we never saw it.

The downside to the use of such ammunition was that it fired a bullet at a considerably lower velocity than standard, drastically affecting both range and accuracy. As an example, the drop in trajectory of a 7.92 mm sub-sonic Mauser bullet is around 16 *feet* at 300 yards compared to the 14 inches of a standard high-velocity bullet at the same range. In practical terms this reduces the effective accurate shooting range of sub-sonic to under 100 yards, hardly sniping range. It would be fine perhaps for very close-range shooting in built-up areas but useless for anything at greater distances.

Camouflage and Kit

The young snipers were excited eventually to have been issued with their rifles as well as being given expert instruction in how to become proficient in their use. This was just a part of their education, though, for aside from being able to shoot accurately, the second most important skill for them to master was to learn the black art of camouflage.

> Every day at sniper school one piece of information was repeated until it engraved itself on my mind. 'NEVER UNDERESTIMATE AN ENEMY SNIPER!' and I do believe that remembering that helped me to survive a grim campaign. Nothing was more true than their ability to blend seamlessly into the landscape. Camouflage for snipers is vital and generally speaking it does not revolve around the typically seen slap-on smears of camouflage cream used on TV and films because that is laughable and wouldn't fool anybody. Good camouflage is a real art and is worth a chapter all to itself and, even then, it would only indicate part of the theme. As an example, in the Normandy hedgerows, [a German's] poor face camouflage cost him dearly.[21] But it was a salutary lesson for me too from that exact moment, because I changed my own facial camouflage to shaded striping ... and in addition I made sure I mostly used a ragged hessian face mask with a ripped netting cover fastened with burlap rags. His error was a severe lesson I took to heart from then onwards. It was my good luck that I was already in position when he tried to hunker down. In just about every phase of the fighting in north-

> Western Europe, I was careful to camouflage my face and hands, I also often wore gloves in which I could uncover my trigger finger for a more sensitive controlled pressure. If not, [hands] were always blackened. I did not daub my face as you'll frequently see of soldiers … daubing does not hide the face from a competent observer. I followed the inspiration of a Tiger's striped camouflage which is far more deceptive, although I striped my face with whatever I could find, such as the black from the cook's pan bottoms as the Max Factor-made camouflage creams were not readily available during the fighting, although I still made use of a ragged net with attached scrim over my face as well. I did try to make a face mask similar to those used by German snipers, but they are very uncomfortable and insects get inside and you sweat even more.

The face paint was the cause of much amusement to the snipers, Harry recalled some of his comrades enacting an impromptu war-dance having smeared their cheeks with green and brown paint. Doubtless, this was not the first time the long-suffering instructors had seen it. Often charcoal from a fire was the only form of face and hand covering available.

Harry added that the Germans used a simple but effective form of head cover that was new to the British snipers:

> A useful device that we came across in Normandy was a wire cage they attached to their shoulders and thoroughly camouflaged. The advantage of a cage was that the sniper could rotate his head within the cage without showing any movement. The idea worked well for them and at times we used the same technique.

As the Allies advanced, cages were frequently found in sniping positions abandoned by the Germans, and British snipers began to copy the idea where it proved appropriate. Good camouflage was what stood between living and dying for a combat sniper and its use needed to be mastered as perfectly as was possible. A properly camouflaged sniper should be capable of lying in undergrowth five feet from an observer without being seen. Not until he was in combat did Harry appreciate just how important personal camouflage was, stating unequivocally that 'it made the difference between life and death'.

Unlike ordinary infantrymen, who were limited by what was available from stores, the snipers were allowed to pick and choose from anything they could get hold of or improvise. Headgear worn in the field, for example, could be a motley selection of woollen cap comforters, scrim scarves, steel helmets or even berets, though Harry had a sensible preference for the helmet, a decision which was later to save his life. In action he wore a net over his helmet and wove camouflaged lengths of hessian, a jute-based loose woven material, through it to break up the outline. He also had a face veil of thin cloth strips that hung over the front brim, which permitted easy use of the scope but covered the rest of his face. Uniforms were covered in foliage when possible, looping it through epaulettes, belts, pack-straps and helmet mesh. This was by no means the end of it, for rifles had to be bound with coloured cloth, usually brown, green and black hessian strips, to break up their regular outline, as nothing in nature is ever regular. Depending on where the sun was, the lenses of the telescopic sight, telescope or binoculars also needed to be covered to prevent them flashing in sunlight. The loose weave net scarf was ideal for this, allowing the sniper to see reasonably clearly through his optics whilst shielding the lens. In urban sniping, Harry adopted the tried and tested method of tying sandbags over his boots and gaiters, as it 'disguised their shape and cut down on the noise of boot-studs on pavements'. He always left the top buttons open on his battledress, wearing a tucked-in green scrim face veil as a scarf, which helped catch sweat and stop insects from crawling inside. Indeed, few people would ever give sweating a thought, but for the snipers it was quite a significant issue in warm weather, as Harry pointed out:

> Sweating is a definite problem for soldiers in the stress of combat, and infantrymen can easily wipe their faces. But snipers must restrict their movements at all times and cannot allow perspiration to interfere with using their optics. For a while I tried using a roughly made eye-cup to aid eye-relief but heat from the eye can mist up a scope

even in hot weather so in combat I left it off but I did keep using a roughly made hessian lens shade on my objective lens to prevent any glints giving me away, and it also kept raindrops off the lens too.

No special camouflaged military clothing was in production early in the war, so snipers simply made use of their battledress with multi-purpose scrim scarves, coloured sacking strips and local vegetation attached to home-made ghillie suits. A few factory-made ghillie suits were kept at headquarters and when needed could be issued to a sniper who required one. These specialist items of clothing were to prove highly effective for the British snipers and comprised a sleeved, knee-length, loose-fitting robe with a hood and it was named after its invention in the nineteenth century by Scottish ghillies for stalking deer in the Highlands; the snipers made up their own variants according to preference. Harry's was of hessian with loops of ribbon sewn onto it, in which cloth or any local flora could be inserted. There were also matching trousers of a deliberately baggy cut that could easily be pulled on over boots and trousers. Harry commented of the ghillie suits, 'They were bulky things to carry and only some were available' at the time of D-Day, indicating that the snipers at that time rarely needed to wear one as a matter of course. After the landings, as the Allies worked their way inland, this all changed as they advanced into the *bocage* country. Harry said of his own ghillie suit that,

> As it happened, I did not receive my personal suit until the [Normandy] breakout, but I found it extremely useful later when we fought through the heavily wooded areas.

Urban fighting did not require effective camouflage so much as swift reflexes. When camouflage was not in use snipers simply wore their ordinary battledress top and trousers, but with all insignia removed. Specifically, the marksman's crossed rifles were never worn in the field.

> We never, ever wore specialist insignia on our battledress, aside from being our death-warrant if captured, it could give the Germans a clue about who was working in the

area. We even removed our divisional insignia and I don't think any battlefield sniper ever made the mistake of having an identifying badge. I only had my sniper's rifles sewn onto my battledress at the end of the war, when I also put up my wound stripe.

Whilst Harry was still in the UK training, an important item of clothing appeared, the camouflaged Denison smock. Introduced in November 1942 for parachutists, it was the first officially manufactured item of camouflage clothing ever issued in the British Army. It was produced in response to a similar, loose garment worn by German parachutists, darkly known as 'the bone sack'. The Denison was to become such a fundamental part of the sniper's uniform, indeed almost a signature item, that it is worth describing in more detail. It was a true smock, in that it had to be pulled over the head to put on; it had a short neck zip, four large practical external patch pockets, button-down shoulder straps and a very distinctive crutch strap which was sewn in place at the rear but could be pulled under the crutch and secured to the front by press studs to stop it from billowing when parachuting. In reality, the parachute harness always prevented this and the strap was there really to stop the garment from creeping up when the harness was put on. Originally the strap was designed to be cut off once no longer required, but later patterns had press studs at the rear as well, so it could be clipped out of the way. Unsurprisingly these were known variously as 'monkey tails', 'donkey tails' and other slightly cruder epithets, but very usefully for the snipers, they also stopped the smock from riding up or twisting when they were crawling. The early production smocks were made of a plain, pale brown cotton cloth and hand-dyed, as at the time there were no looms available that could create a camouflage pattern. By 1943 this had been remedied but until the end of the war, every bolt of cloth had a different coloured weave, so no two Denisons were identical. It had its drawbacks, though, and Harry said of it:

> The smock was a wonderful garment, despite not having been designed for snipers, but it was not waterproof and became very heavy in the rain. The loose fit of the sleeves

A very early 1st Pattern Denison smock, one of the hand-dyed examples produced before looms were designed that were able to provide camouflage material. This one has a maker's label: 'Wareings, N'ton [Northampton] Ltd' and is dated 1942. It has a short neck zip and woollen cuffs. The crutch strap is visible at the bottom and was held in place, depending on the length required, by any pair of the six press studs seen on the lower front panel.

gave no purchase for the sniper sling when worn on the left arm, and most of us sewed a brass hook or large button to the rear of the left upper arm to hold the sling in place. I also had a long, thin waterproof pouch sewn into the rear left of my smock so I could lie on my stomach, and still reach my observation telescope. I never used the leather carry-cases for either my scope or binoculars, preferring to carry them inside my smock. Because of the amount of crawling that we did, and the rough ground we were often concealed in, smocks tore and wore holes quickly, and a seasoned sniper could always be recognised by the odd patches sewn onto his Denison. As supplies of smocks came through, they were often grabbed by officers who coveted them as well. A coverall was available that was issued to tank crews for maintenance tasks and our Divisional Camouflage Pool officer and his staff took batches and roughly crack-painted them (grey, brown, green) and handed them around to the sniper sections. A similar painted coverall was given to me by the Camouflage Pool sergeant, but he had improved it with sewn-on webbing straps into which I could add local camouflage, and he had sewn over it all ragged bits of scrim. It was my first ghillie smock, but I only received it as we were clearing up in Normandy; it came too late for my hedgerow sniping operations.

In 1944 I was issued with this complete camouflage suit. A smock and trousers of a very unusual disruptive pattern that I have never seen since,[22] so I presume it may well have been a prototype sniper's suit I was trying out ... it was in addition wind proof and I found it very useful indeed, as snipers get very cold and are unable to move about to get circulation going. In action I wore my complete camouflage coverall [Denison] over my battledress.

I frequently wore hessian sandbag covers over each boot, tied with dirty string. It was a help in various ways, it camouflaged my black army boots (oil-dubbined for water resistance and removal of any shine). I tried not to leave boot prints when I roamed forwards as enemy patrols look for such details, and the ragged hessian gave an indistinct spoor, plus it helped prevent slipping as I crossed cobbled areas. Typically, though, I only wore the sandbags when I was in full camouflage, and with painted face and hands under a scrim and ripped green face veil. I did not leave behind any trace, no ejected cartridges for enemy patrols to find and no trail. I did wear webbing, mainly because of the weight carried of various needed attachments, it was green-blancoed, my gaiters were green and all metalwork was painted drab olive green. We only cleaned off the paint after the ceasefire and we were given permission to paint our rifles if we chose to do so. Some Scottish regimental snipers did paint their rifles, but most didn't and used camouflage wrapping. I decided that I'd always keep my rifle and TS wrapped in scrim. I removed the scrim frequently ... (it) got wet and stayed wet for long periods at a time and it eventually took the deep black colour off the TS and rifle action, which couldn't be helped.

Regarding my ammunition, I very rarely wore the web ammunition pouches as they were far too bulky for any operational sniper who has to crawl flattened long distances as a matter of course. So I carried ordinary ball ammunition, which my rifle was zeroed for, in my right Denison pocket and spare armour-piercing and incendiary separated out in other pockets but typically, snipers do not shoot too much if they hope to survive. I also carried a .38-inch Webley revolver in a holster. I always wore this on my right side on a web belt, with my holster fastened to another small pouch with spare .38 in. ammo and another small web ammo pouch with my compass.

Also supplied in considerable numbers was a simple white winter over-smock of a type virtually identical to that issued in the First World War. It was made of thin cotton, had a drawstring hood, four patch pockets and loose trousers with an adjustable waistband. It was designed to go over the top of the battledress, but as Harry pointed out, it was nowhere near warm enough for winter, and the largest sizes were always selected by the snipers, so that they could be pulled on over a Denison. Harry found it very useful in Holland, complementing it with white field-dressing bandage wrapped around his rifle and scope, and a home-made mask made from a piece of bed sheet 'liberated' from a nearby house. He always wore his helmet, although he eschewed the white paint that some snipers used. But he added some important finishing touches:

> These were very loose garments that slipped over our normal battledress, in fact mine was easily big enough to go over my Denison. We bound our rifles in white bandage and I had a white coverall on my helmet with white strands hanging down to cover as much of my face as possible. A pure white smock would stand out too much, as the fields were never purely one colour, so we added splodges of black or brown here and there both on the smocks and our rifles and helmets. In a hedgerow or treeline, you were very well camouflaged but we were not given white gloves for some reason. It was too cold not to wear gloves, so we devised different solutions. Some got hold of DRs' [Despatch Riders'] gauntlets which were very long and warm but made of brown leather, so they cut the cuffs down and used white paint on them. I had some green wool gloves which I wrapped bandage round, but later managed to get a pair of light-coloured woollen gloves that were a sort of mitt but with a separate trigger finger. I'm not sure if they were British or Canadian, but they were very practical.

He often carried his entrenching tool in its web pouch which he wore behind him and whenever necessary would use it to scrape a shallow pit from which to shoot. Occasionally, if he was to be concealed for a day or two, another sniper would come with him carrying a proper shovel, and they would dig a slit trench, then camouflage Harry inside it before leaving. This was both secure and well hidden, but at the cost of being impossible to leave for any reason during daylight hours. Highly unpleasant as Harry pointed out, when one had 'a bad case of the trots'.

> Two water bottles were always carried by myself, and many other snipers. But never attached to our webbing harness. We carried them loosely with long thin web straps just slung across our backs. Drinking water was vital … but I might find myself lying prone with my rifle barrel over soft soil or sand, so with great caution I would wet the ground beneath my rifle muzzle, otherwise on firing it disturbed the top layer which could raise dust, which in turn could be spotted by an expert observer.

Sniper Training and Equipment

Water was obviously a necessity, but so was food and in this respect the snipers did not fare as well as the infantry for most of the time. They often went on patrol in the very early mornings or late evenings, leaving before the cooks had prepared hot food for the infantry, and coming back late when there was seldom anything hot left to eat. When in a hide Harry could only eat what he could carry so much of his service was spent eating cold food, which he believed resulted in later trouble with his digestion.

> I never carried a lot of food, typically hardtack biscuits and hard black chocolate lumps. At times I obtained self-heating tins of soup or stew but great care was needed with these tins as they could explode if not vented properly with the tip of my Fairbairn-Sykes knife. Sniping is intensely stressful and water was of course vitally important and often in short supply, but my bottles only ever had water in them, never spirits. I never ever took the offered rum ration either. I had to keep my wits about me when forward, so rum was definitely out of the question. I am a lifelong non-smoker and I refused to work with any smoker who might give our position away, hence I mostly operated alone with my colonel's permission.

In reality, what the army provided for the snipers often proved to be less than effective in combat and the Pattern 1907 leather sling was a case in point. It was a complicated design made for firing on a target range, taking the whole weight of the rifle and providing a firm platform for the shooter's left arm. This was perfectly fine in civilian marksmanship competitions, but when the sling was issued in WWI, it was realised that, when it was wet, it became too slippery to be usable and unless dried very carefully, the leather split, eventually rendering it useless. Exhibiting the care which he lavished on all his equipment, Harry wrote:

> It is true they became slippery when wet and took a long time to dry out; we couldn't hurry by drying with heat as it cracked them. I had no problems with stickiness as my sling was always wrapped in hessian anyway, but I regularly cleaned it with saddle soap. The brass became green so

> the British government ordered a special batch from the US ... with chemically blackened hooks. Some snipers had a personal preference for the longer Bren gun webbing slings. Shortly before the war ended a small supply of British-made webbing slings, a basic copy of the American one, trickled over, but I never got one.

Such was his attention to detail that Harry even removed the leather strap of his binoculars and replaced it with a thin green webbing one, which was unaffected by rain. However, there was an unexpected consequence of being perfectly camouflaged on the battlefield, for snipers were invisible to both sides, specifically advancing armoured vehicles. The *bocage* hedgerows were so thick that Allied tanks were modified with a series of sharp horizontal blades welded on the front[23] that they used to slice their way at speed through the hedges – and this was an effective tactic often used to deal with enemy snipers. Harry commented that all snipers were terrified of being crushed by one, as generally their slit trenches or hides were not deep enough to provide protection in the event of being run over and he added that some quick method of evacuating the hide was always prepared, in case the dreaded rumble and squeak of an approaching vehicle was heard.

Concealment, Decoys and Intelligence

Blending in with the surrounding countryside was all very well, but the snipers also needed to learn where *not* to place themselves for observation or shooting. In open country, especially in sites that the enemy could overlook, a foxhole would be prepared at night then covered with suitable undergrowth and, whenever possible, built with two exits running from it. Using a foxhole, or 'hide' was the most common form of concealment, but provided only minimal protection if discovered, hence the creation of a quick escape route. Later in the campaign, Harry was to find this out uncomfortably for himself. Care had to be exercised with the ground in front of the hide, for as Harry has mentioned, the muzzle blast of the rifle could raise a cloud of dust or leaf debris. Placing a lightly filled and well camouflaged sandbag under the muzzle was one solution, as was carefully removing any debris that could be disturbed and pouring water on loose soil. The sniper would enter before first light and make himself as comfortable as possible, no easy task in view of biting insects, heat or cold and the need to keep drinking to avoid dehydrating, with the inevitable requirement to urinate as well. Any movement had to be an absolute minimum and undertaken very slowly. A sniper was never sure if he was under observation and instructors went to great pains to point out that if there was an experienced observer, even the twitch of a branch on a still morning could bring fatal retribution. In training, the selection of sites for hides was covered in great detail since, as one instructor commented, 'A hide could become your grave if you do not get it right.' It was a statement Harry took to heart and he always chose his positions with extreme care and he disliked any hide that had only one entry/exit.

There were also external factors that had to be taken into account, some of which were completely out of the control of the snipers. The instructors specifically warned against choosing anywhere where there were animals, for example.

> Every place had its dangers, some more so than others ... your position could be given away unintentionally even by animals, and all snipers were particularly wary of animals. It doesn't matter if they are wild, domestic or farm animals, for all are curious and will approach soldiers on the ground in camouflaged positions. Such attention is a dead give-away to a skilled enemy observer who watches for such things.

Birds such as rooks and crows were particularly sensitive to intruders and would flock and alarm call if someone was in cover nearby. Harry recalled reading as a boy a World War One memoir by an Australian sniper[24] who killed a persistent Turkish marksman because a single lark was flying above him in a wheat field, trilling in alarm, a story that he said he always bore in mind. Snipers were further warned not to make use of any obvious places such as stand-alone clumps of hedgerow, bushes or haystacks: advice Harry once ignored to his cost, as he later recounts. Even long hedges bordering fields were dangerous if cattle were grazing nearby as they were always curious about humans.

After finding on one occasion what he believed was a particularly good hide in the roof of a large barn, he gradually became aware of a commotion around him. Unwittingly, he had settled very near a rafter on which swallows had built a nest, and the parents were wheeling and swooping in alarm, crying shrilly. He knew that the commotion and movement would draw the attention of any observer. So, very gradually, he lowered himself down from his perch, crept out of the rear of the barn and began the search once again for a good place of concealment.

> Even if there are dead animals around, the rest of a cattle herd will continue to graze and will only become curious about something live in the vicinity, such as a sniper.

Harry noted that, when on operations, if he had found a near-ideal place in which to hide, he occasionally had to kill an overly persistent animal 'as quietly as possible' usually with the Fairbairn-Sykes dagger that he carried. He also made a point of mentioning that cold weather brought its own specific problems. Aside from the danger of the hot gases being visible in still air after a rifle shot, there was a more subtle danger that could lead to discovery. Not only animals, but the weather also played a crucial part.

> Bitter cold in particular requires special awareness. A perfect example is that well-trained observers … can often detect warm breath pluming upward. If a concealed sniper speaks with his companion, they must both be extremely careful that their breathing does not reveal their position.

Woods were ideal for concealment, with plenty of natural cover and some protection from small-arms fire, but British snipers were told repeatedly never to climb trees for sniping. Instructors pointed out that there was only one quick way down from a tree and that was vertically and likely dead. Japanese, German and Soviet snipers were all taught how to make use of trees, but Harry was dubious that experienced German snipers in Normandy actually did so. He only ever saw one example of tree-sniping, which is described later.

> It is feasible that some ordinary German riflemen made the mistake of firing from tree-tops but it is hardly likely that a

trained sniper would do so, again because it is so obvious and no one has a quick retreat from such a position.

Of course, much fighting after D-Day was through towns and villages and these presented their own problems. There were many potentially inviting places for a sniper to conceal himself, but some were simply death-traps:

> We were taught *never* to use such obvious places as [church] bell-towers, which the Germans often did. It was common practice for British troops to bring up an anti-tank gun to blow away the steeple tops, though they were often subsequently used for our artillery observers who sent back radio information.

The training in Britain included access to empty villages whose occupants had been unceremoniously evacuated at short notice by the army. This provided the snipers and infantrymen with a sense of how difficult it was to fight in such a closed environment. All of the instructors laboured the point repeatedly that far from being a wasteland, the more rubble that was on the ground in a built-up area, the harder it became to spot and deal with snipers. This was particularly true in bigger cities, where networks of sewers or tunnels enabled snipers of both sides to move covertly from hide to hide. This was proven in practice when the Allied troops got into Caen, which had unfortunately been reduced to rubble by British bombing, and Harry saw for himself how failure to understand the complexity of city fighting could lead to death.

> Bomb damage caused us real trouble ... the entire area was turned into rubble, all perfect hiding places for the German ... snipers who had quickly moved into position thus causing the Allied attacking troops severe casualties. The German snipers moved all the time between the damaged remains of the town's buildings, so they were particularly hard to locate. Those [Allied troops] who fought later inside Germany itself came up against the same problems of having to fight their way through mounds of rubble and once again the German snipers exacted a very heavy toll.

Many of these Germans were veterans of the Eastern Front and had, between them, notched up thousands of kills. They were both highly experienced and highly motivated by their determination to prevent Allied troops setting foot on German soil. The trainee British snipers were taught always to use deep shadows inside ruined buildings to observe and snipe from, as this supposedly rendered them undetectable to even the most keen-eyed enemy, although later Harry found this was not always the case. Despite many newspaper photos showing snipers sitting at a window to shoot these, like so many contemporary images, were done purely for publicity for in reality to shoot in this manner meant the sniper was effectively signing his own death warrant. However, what was very effective was using a small gap in a shattered wall or between broken roof slates and, when necessary, snipers would carefully ease out a few more loose bricks or tiles to facilitate this. Of course, very great care had to be taken to ensure that when the sniper was in position his point of aim was not directly to the front, from where the muzzle flash of a shot could be spotted. In a supposedly empty house, the slightest unusual movement could prove quite literally, a dead give-away.

British Army doctrine dictated that snipers were expected to work in pairs and, outwardly at least, this was accepted as the official requirement. In reality, there was usually much latitude given by sniping officers as to how snipers wanted to work; Harry did not like being with anyone else and he had the agreement of his commanding officer that he could work alone. Sometimes, though, it was simple common sense to work as a pair, particularly if a lot of observation time was required. The human eye cannot take the constant strain of looking through an optical sight without regular periods of rest and the observers were advised to rest every half an hour, and look at foliage as the muted colours of green and brown helped relax strained eye muscles. Harry was unusual, however, as most of the others in his section preferred to work in pairs. As he said, 'It made my life harder, but I always believed it was also safer.' As to choosing what and when to shoot, this was left entirely to the individual, as there could never be any hard and fast rules applied. Often he had a choice between possibly giving away his position

Sniper Training and Equipment

by taking the chance of a shot, or forgoing shooting to continue quietly observing. Harry's later account of shooting a high-ranking German officer is an excellent case in point:

> Often, we were able to identify rank with our Scout Regiment telescopes ... but signs of rank were not always visible, especially with the Waffen-SS who 'dressed down' and did not always display rank or decorations, but the manner of their bearing with their troops often gave us a good idea of who was in charge. Target identification is vital to all snipers, and we knew from our training that little things give away the officers. Soldiers bearing the red cross signs such as stretcher bearers were not fired upon if they came to collect dead bodies but anyone else was a fair target and mostly engaged by a follow-up shot. There was of course a major difficulty in knowing for certain if a shot fired had killed outright, or severely wounded the soldier ... even at times if the shot had been a very near miss, for highly trained soldiers will drop to the ground and then roll to another position if grazed or wounded. Those who remained completely immobile for long afterwards, we could be certain they had been eliminated from battle completely. When we spotted an enemy patrol that we decided to engage, the rule was to go for the radio operator first, otherwise he will call in artillery on you ... then the officer or NCO in charge, then move your position as quietly as possible. Maybe later you will get another shot at the leaderless patrol from your pre-chosen alternative position.

One area of sniping that is seldom covered is the use of decoys to try and fool enemy snipers into giving away their positions by shooting, whilst being carefully observed. Harry devoted quite a lot of text to explaining how this system worked and the salient points are repeated here.

> By the time our joint invasion forces landed in Normandy ... decoy dummies had been made up and a limited supply came over soon after the initial assault landings. Each division had appointed a Camouflage Pool officer who had

a few NCO craftsmen and several lower ranks to make up specialised camouflage units. The main task of these units was to devise and build any type of camouflage nets or devices to fill whatever requests they received. As a sideline these units offered their skills to any specialists who might find their products useful. It was a bonus to us that the Camouflage Pool also supplied various types of Denison camo smocks.

Really good and well camouflaged decoys came into use ... to seriously deceive sniper observers into believing that weak positions were heavily defended. The game became really cat-and-mouse and we snipers resorted to our 22× spotting scopes in an attempt to figure out exactly what we were seeing. My battalion had some dummy-type decoys dressed in battle blouse and web equipment. They were lifelike with covered strips in their helmets and they passed well for real soldiers even at short hedgerow ranges. At dawn and twilight, we had some successes with our own 'smoking soldiers' which simply consisted of sticking a lighted cigarette in a dummy's mouth. When employing individual dummies, we would tie netting and scrim on ... and even fasten rifles to appear as if they were being held. The operators had to move a dummy in a manner that would appear to an enemy sniper to be a careless or casual mistake by a living soldier.

A useful technique that might trap an inexperienced sniper was to place decoys closer to your own lines than your hide. In that way an enemy might be induced to crawl too close to your own lines because he was concentrating on the dummy.

A poor decoy is worse than no decoy. Everyone seemed to realise that, and the quality of the decoys we received was of a high standard. Snipers are astute fighting men and if they spotted a decoy, they ignored it and were then inclined to search diligently for the concealed sniper they knew must be nearby.

Harry's snipers sometimes used fake radio sets with long aerials placed as though they were in a command or communication

vehicle, or sometimes a little smoke from a staged fire that looked as though someone was being careless. This could bring down completely wasted artillery, mortar or machine-gun fire and as a result enemy gun emplacements could be spotted, but most importantly it would more often draw German sniper attention. Harry commented that 'We were able to add to our battalion's tally' as a result of clever decoy use. The British were not the only ones to make good use of dummies, though, for the German snipers were extremely cunning and at times also showed a sense of humour.

> We had advanced to a German line, where it was reported a movement was seen, so we crept up to observe. It appeared to be an arm waving, so we reported back that we thought it was a decoy. The Bren gunners were sent out and they riddled it, but it kept waving. When we eventually approached it, it was a dummy, in a uniform top and helmet, absolutely shredded by the bullets, the arm being moved by a string and counterweight. The head was a sandbag with a smiling face painted on it.

Shooting individual enemy soldiers rarely had any effect on the outcome of a battle, but good intelligence could – so having been taught when and where to shoot from, the snipers were then instructed on *not* shooting, but simply observing, which seemed something of a paradox. They were inculcated into the complexities of intelligence-gathering, which by 1942 was already becoming one of the most highly valued battlefield functions of a sniper. The old days of firing at any suitable target were long past, and it was stressed that what was now regarded as far more vital was the unique role a sniper could play in reporting on enemy movements and strength. If well-concealed, then shooting at tempting targets was mostly a waste of their special skills unless there were very special circumstances, as after firing the sniper would be forced to move position.

What they learned and reported back to the IO was regarded as secret and they were warned of the dangers of talking to any of their own battalion infantrymen about what they did or saw.

> It was quite a rigid ruling that snipers kept to themselves, and they were ordered not to discuss their role even with their mates in the rifle companies. This was to ensure that details of their [sniper] operations, equipment in use, tactics etc., could not be revealed under interrogation by soldiers later captured ... for such information was always sought by each side as a matter of importance due to the constant losses of officers and senior NCOs due to snipers. We had orders ... that the intelligence that we gathered in the course of sniper patrols was only to be discussed with our own senior officers and the Battalion 'I' Section who quickly forwarded all useful information to rear HQ Intelligence.

All snipers kept personal log books detailing kills and observations, but it was utterly forbidden for these to be carried on operations. The only notebook carried was one in which were recorded:

> ... any relevant details we observed on our patrols, such as shots fired and possible results, times of such incidents, recognition of enemy units from uniform insignia, enemy movements, heavy weapons, any type of tracked or wheeled transport, results of our shelling or mortar fire. Map references had to be given for each item noted. Plus, anything else we saw that might be of possible use to our own Battalion 'I' officer.

Harry also remarked that all entries had to be started afresh every day, old ones were torn out, and they were all written in block capitals so no report could ever be misread by anyone. Of course, such observational work required considerable proficiency in map reading and a complete mastery of the prismatic compass, hence the stress placed on the topic in training. Harry commented that:

> If you asked a Brigade Intelligence officer what he considered of prime importance, a high body count from snipers or highly detailed military intelligence, he would undoubtedly tell you that first and foremost he wanted information. In fact, the CO told me that whatever we had learned at sniper school, I was to work to his direct wishes. He told me he had

> no interest in me targeting any and every enemy soldier; his orders were to supply first, as much fresh field intelligence as possible, with field sketches, estimated distances, if any water obstacles were fordable, and anything which looked as if it was camouflaged etc. In terms of shooting, I was only to concentrate on 'priority' targets: officers, NCOs, radiomen and so on. [I was] to ignore private soldiers unless they were a danger to me.

What optical equipment was used by the snipers was determined by the distances at which the enemy were from their hide, and how much detailed information was needed. The issue 6×30 binoculars were perfectly adequate despite their slightly low magnification, as they provided a wide field of view as well as being easy to carry. Conversely, the big three-draw Scout Telescope provided tremendous power, but was very tiring to use for any period of time and not so easy to carry. Harry believed both had their rightful place on the battlefield.

> For general observation and a wide field of view, the binoculars were good and not as hard on the eyes as the Scout Telescope which was incomparable for seeing great distances. I did obtain a pair of very good German Zeiss binoculars which were more powerful than our own and I resisted all attempts to be parted from them. The Scout Telescope was hard on the eyes, though, and required regular rests to prevent eye-strain which resulted in bad headaches.

The deliberately hard weeks of training were intended to equip the snipers with the skills they required to become effective and to survive. Once their training had finished and they had passed the final exams, they found there was no let-up in their schedules. Elite as they were, the snipers were in reality just a small cog in a very large military wheel and, first and foremost, they were infantry soldiers, albeit highly specialised ones. So, they had to learn to work efficiently with all the other branches of the army: armoured, artillery and infantry, and to co-operate and co-ordinate with them whenever it was necessary to launch an attack at battalion or corps level. So they trained and trained, and sometimes Harry caught a glimpse of just what an incredible fighting machine he was a part of.

> [Infantry] moving forward into an attack was a formidable sight. You just couldn't help but feel the thrill run down your back, it was a mixture of exhilaration which combined with an internal, nagging fear of the consequences. I can still see it in my mind's eye quite clearly even after all these years, for before first light all the companies moved into position on our start lines. I operated mostly with the companies designated as our lead assault troops, close behind [was] a third company ready to leap-frog past as the first attacking companies reached their initial objectives. The support company followed ready to set up their mortars and anti-tank guns ... to be ready for expected enemy counter attacks, whilst one company took its turn as being the reserve ready to rush forwards to take over as required. [The artillery] was all very carefully timed so that it changed into a creeping barrage with shells falling just ahead as we advanced. Our tank support started up and attacking companies tucked themselves behind them ... once the Crocodile[25] flame-throwing tanks opened up the companies moved in extended formation whenever possible.
>
> For us battalion snipers, it was our task to move forwards in pairs with each company, but we worked from flank positions, keeping pace as best we could to pin down and eliminate priority targets ... above all enemy snipers who would be after our own officers and NCOs. During attacks the fact that we had to move fast meant that calculated risks had to be taken, for we were only too well aware that enemy snipers would have our own supporting snipers at the top of their priority list too. Depending on the type of attack action, it sometimes happened that our snipers were held in reserve until our forward platoons had reached their first objectives, then we rushed forwards to take up positions to engage the enemy on their first counter-attack.

> Positions taken had to be quickly consolidated, but always with the prior knowledge that we were always prepared to continue the advance for two reasons. One was to take advantage of the battle situation to gain more ground and better positions, plus we had to allow for the possibility that the enemy would know the range to an inch … to lay down a highly accurate barrage on the positions we had just taken.

In addition, repeated practice amphibious landings were made on south coast beaches as well as assaults over open country and in the sunken, shrouded back lanes of Dorset and Devon, the nearest that could be found to the *bocage* country of Normandy, although this destination was as yet unknown to the soldiers. Harry had a little to say on the training:

> It was repetitive but we knew it would prove useful. There had been a lot of intelligence gathered from resistance units in France, as well as air reconnaissance photos. As snipers, we were fortunate in some ways, as we were excluded from a lot of infantry tactical training. Instead, we were given special instruction on identifying targets, such as camouflaged MG positions, anti-tank guns, other snipers and so forth. Our job was to try and pave the way for the infantry by dealing with any probable threats before they began to hold up our advance. This often meant getting ahead of the attack to take up suitable positions. We were under no illusions that this was going to be extremely hazardous.

All through his training, Harry had been a lance-corporal, but he was pleased to be informed that he was to be promoted to full corporal, although he didn't have time to sew on his new insignia before they embarked on the transport ship prior to the landings. In fact, he said it was many weeks before he was given his new stripes but as he wore no rank or insignia on his combat battledress, he didn't think it made any difference! He eventually did sew them onto his uniform, but not until he was in Germany and shortly afterwards was promoted to sergeant anyway!

Chapter 3

D-Day and Into the *Bocage*

REVEILLE FOR THE GREEN HOWARDS on the morning of 6 June 1944 was around 2:30 a.m. on board the transport MS *Empire Lance*. The sea was choppy and many soldiers were suffering badly as a result, ignoring calls for breakfast. At 5 a.m. they began to transfer to their LCAs (Landing Craft Assault) which was no easy matter as the boats rose and fell several feet in the high swell. Essential kit and uncountable boxes of ammunition had already been loaded the night before. One by one, the LCAs pulled away from the transport and headed towards the distant shoreline. The unit was part of XXX Corps, which included Harry's 50th Infantry Division, the 49th Infantry Division and 7th Armoured Division.

This corps had been specifically selected to spearhead the assault, as the fighting qualities of its infantry were believed to be second to none. Many had seen service in North Africa and Italy and there were a lot of seasoned troops in the ranks. Their disembarkation point was Gold Beach, the first objective being the town of Ver-sur-Mer. The division was expected to fight inland and capture the ground from Bayeux in the west to St-Léger in the east. This was considered of extreme importance as it included the main transport route to Caen, a vital supply line for the Germans. In the event, they would capture more German-held ground than any other formation on D-Day, advancing seven miles inland.

At 7.37 a.m. Harry's landing craft crunched unexpectedly onto a sandbar some distance from the intended beach and, lurching horribly in the heavy swell, began disgorging its living but rather sea-sick cargo of soldiers of 6th Battalion, Green Howards. They were much further out to sea than expected, but with their LCA stuck on the sandbar and heavy incoming fire being aimed at it, the men had no option but to drop off the ramp into the freezing sea as fast as possible.

> We went in earlier than planned as we had been circling in our LCA awhile in very heavy waves which were caused by the battleships side-on firing all their heavy guns. The LCA I was in hit a sandbank way out and we went in fully-laden neck deep, although my 4T was well wrapped in waterproofs and my telescope had condoms knotted over all the optical surfaces, as well as the barrel etc. – but it hadn't kept the water out. I waded ashore with the first assault waves, struggling under the weight of my 80-pound pack in water up to my neck. It was very slow going, the seafloor was uneven and the [blast from the] heavy naval guns meant that we were swamped by big waves and the noise was indescribable. I was surprised at how many soldiers there were already on the beach, as I expected we would be among the first. Everything was soaked through with seawater … [including] my Scout Regiment telescope, binoculars, compass and watch by the time I actually reached Gold. I was worried if the salt water had given me a problem but … later … I washed all the optical surfaces under a farmhouse tap in an attempt to save them. But everything I wore was still soaking wet at dusk. I was fortunate, though, as many men jumped into deeper water and were drowned under the weight of their kit.

The sniper section staggered up the sliding shingle under their heavy equipment but the crack and ping of bullets passing close by were barely audible in the general cacophony of the ripping sound of the MG 42 machine guns,[1] the firework crackle of small-arms fire and the crashing mortar and artillery rounds. Harry commented that at no point could he determine where any fire was actually coming from. Around him, men killed outright dropped like sacks, some floating face down at the water's edge, others motionless on the ground. He gritted his teeth and headed up the beach towards the low wall that bordered the road. Razor-sharp clouds of bullet-shattered pebbles flew upwards from impacting bullets and all the soldiers hunched down to try and make themselves smaller targets.

Harry had already loaded his rifle and put the safety catch on, and now he fired into the sand to clear the barrel – just in front of an officer who was in battledress but wearing a naval peaked cap. It just so happened that this was the Beachmaster, who was responsible for ensuring everything arrived where it should and that the troops promptly moved off the shore towards their objectives. All the men had been warned not to stop under any circumstances to take cover, as it would prove virtually impossible to get the advance moving again. The officer shouted something quite rude at Harry, and motioned for him to get out of his sight as quickly as possible. Harry took little notice of him, trying instead to follow the marked route made safe by Royal Engineer mine-clearance teams.

This event had a very curious postscript some fifty years later, when Harry somewhat reluctantly went to France to attend a D-Day anniversary and found himself standing in a hotel bar with some old comrades. Behind him, sitting at a table with maps spread out and a group around him listening intently, was none other than the former Beachmaster. Someone asked how close he had got to being shot by the Germans and he responded by saying the nearest he actually got to being killed was by a 'bloody silly sod who nearly shot me firing his rifle by mistake'. At this point Harry introduced himself as that very man, pointing out there was absolutely no mistake involved. Apparently, they later parted very amicably.

Crouching in the lee of the seafront wall to regain his breath, Harry took stock. Most of his section were visible, so he lifted his right arm and pointed to the buildings immediately across the road, pulled himself upright and sprinted as fast as his waterlogged uniform and equipment would allow, which he admitted was not quite so much a run as a series of controlled lurches.

> With my pack soaked with seawater I stumbled rather than ran off the beach towards the seafront. There were fast-firing Spandau machine guns and mortars all around me and I do vividly recall burying my head into the legs of a dead German soldier as protection at some point. We had been warned to get off the beach as fast as possible, otherwise the assault could fail if the Germans managed to gather the reinforcements they needed to mount a counter-attack,

which we could not have held off. Our initial objective was simply to reach the road running parallel to the beach.

At this juncture, Harry had not yet refitted the scope to his rifle, knowing that at the very short ranges involved in street fighting, it would be useless. This proved to be a wise decision, when a grey-green clad figure ran between a truck and building and Harry instinctively fired a snapshot.

> I used 'Kentucky windage' to aim off and I know my eyes were wet through with water as I fired in anger for the first time. I was never sure if it was because there was sweat pouring down my face or just the seawater dripping from inside my helmet, but the figure was blurred, though I hit him. Later on, I had to jump over the poor sod, he was young and blond and good-looking, with his eyes wide open, staring at nothing. It was the first and last time I ever saw up close someone I had killed. In fact, on D-Day I only fired three times, each time I dropped an NCO, all of whom were running.

Seeing his victim was an experience he vowed never to repeat. There had been much concern by army commanders about how they could keep track of the advancing infantry, when there was no means of contacting them once they landed, and there was the very real danger they could come under fire from ground-strafing Allied aircraft who were unable to discern friend from foe. An idea used during the previous war was resurrected, as Harry explained.

> Someone had the bright idea that each attacking infantry-man should carry on his small pack a small triangle of bright yellow cloth which we were supposed to unfurl and let it hang down behind us to identify us as Allied forces to fast-flying pilots. Whoever thought up this curious idea very obviously had no experience of front-line battle, because there was no way it could work. What it would do instead was to provide a clearer target for enemy marksmen in all that smoke laid down to cover our movements. As for fighter pilots already under terrific anti-aircraft fire themselves, to attempt to spot a yellow triangle as they swooped down

> low and very fast over the beaches was too much to ask; in any case planes start their MG fire ... *before* they reach target areas, so typically it is too late to see tiny warning triangles. I never unfurled mine at all.

He also commented that after landing he witnessed a soldier on fire because one of the phosphorous grenades he was carrying had been hit by enemy fire and exploded. Harry was carrying two of these as well as a pair of No. 36 Mills fragmentation grenades. He elected to keep the Mills bombs but dumped the yellow triangle and phosphorus grenades in someone's front garden.

The fighting was uncoordinated and quite chaotic.

> I seemed to be running around like mad all day and the weather had turned very hot so there was an indescribable stench of dead bodies, both theirs and ours. Later we had the horrible task of wrapping them in blankets and putting them in slit trenches, marking the graves with rifles. I met a Spitfire pilot later who told me he could smell the dead as he flew over. The fighting petered out as it got dark and we gathered near our HQ building for a roll-call. It was depressing as we had had so many casualties; I thought to myself that as a sniper, the odds against me surviving were very slim. Overnight my clothes dried on me and we managed to get hot tea and soup, but very soon everyone began to suffer from dysentery because of the huge swarms of big black flies feeding on the dead. One thing I dared not do was take my wet boots off and it was a week before it became possible. We all had a form of 'trench foot' by then and the MO gave us all special powder to use and we had dry socks issued, as ours spare clothing was still very soggy.

The initial problem for the Allied soldiers had been simply getting off the beach in the face of the heavy small-arms fire directed from well-sited pillboxes. Harry's first objective, Ver-sur-Mer, was reachable only by two small roads which were well defended by flanking machine guns, but the Howards pushed stubbornly forwards, dealing one at a time with the machine guns. Although the landing was tough, the heaviest fighting did not start until 7 June by which time the Germans had moved up reserves, mostly Panzergrenadiers with much combat experience, who fought in close co-operation with their own armoured vehicles. However, the biggest obstacle was not so much the number of Germans (fewer than it could have been because of successful Allied deceptions) but the nature of the countryside itself. It was a mix of small villages, orchards, open farmland and the *bocage* that was traditional to Normandy. Indeed, it is impossible to talk of the invasion without the mention of the *bocage*, a dense region of hedgerows and woods that covered most of the Cherbourg peninsula, and stretched east as far as Falaise and south to Domfront.

Some description of this singular area might be helpful in helping to understand the unique problems faced by Harry and the advancing Allied infantrymen. Geographically it presented the advancing infantry and snipers with their biggest tactical challenge, while at the same time giving the defending Germans a huge advantage. Its characteristic features were the incredibly dense hedgerows, many dating back to Norman times, that could be over twenty feet tall and several feet thick. These were utterly impenetrable to human beings unless paths were blown by explosives or mechanically cut. Only the specially adapted Rhino tanks with blades mounted on their hulls could punch a path through (and these were not available initially). Carefully dug in and camouflaged German snipers operated with impunity from this protection, whilst successfully holding up the advancing allies for hours. It was usually impractical to employ artillery, as the opposing forces were often within a hundred yards or less of each other, and although ordinary tanks were effective, there were seldom enough of them where and when they were needed. Identifying the position of a sniper was virtually impossible for most infantrymen and the only solution was to bring up Allied snipers to flush them out. It was, in Harry's opinion, by far the worst terrain in which he ever had to fight in the entire war. He described it as 'nightmarish' and it placed unimaginable stress on the snipers. When talking about it, there were times he would pause and fall silent, seeing events that were still in his mind's eye. Just occasionally he declined to continue and I never pressed him on the matter.

> I learned a vital lesson in that country though … I was settled into a good position deep inside a high hedge before first signs of daylight, and I watched as a German sniper arrived and started to hunker down in another hedge which was very close to me. His pale face gave him away in the dark leaves, though possibly he intended to fit a face mask as they often did. I never gave him that chance, I fired at his face and he remained motionless. I had fired only once and had seen he was alone … it was a while before I decided to move in case other German soldiers found him, for he was too close for safety [Harry estimated he was less than 100 yards away]. I took careful readings with my compass to make a note of where he could be found and later on I gave those details to our Intelligence officer. We always did that in case one of our patrols could go and collect his TS rifle, to prevent it being used against us again. His pale face cost him dearly and in a way it was a shock-call to me too that I needed to avoid his error.

They continued to advance slowly, for while German resistance in that sector was not as stiff as had been expected, there were still enough defenders to make life very difficult. The Green Howards' snipers were constantly in action, moving up with the infantry and dealing with the many emplaced machine guns.

> We were soon stopped by a machine gun firing in enfilade from a hill above us, so two of us snipers crawled forwards. It was well dug in, but easy to locate because of its tremendous rate of fire and smoke from the barrel. We both decided to shoot simultaneously and the firing stopped abruptly. The infantry moved up quickly past us, and we heard grenades bursting, which seemed to settle the matter.

The many pillboxes overlooking the beaches posed a particularly difficult problem as they were cleverly sited to provide interlocking fields of fire and it was almost impossible to outflank them. Some infantry flame-throwers were available but it was hard for the operators to get close enough to be effective and the only way was to ensure the gunners inside were made to keep their heads down with accurate fire through the embrasures, enabling infantry to get close enough to throw grenades or blast fire-jets through the gunports. The only VC won on D-Day was at Gold Beach by veteran soldier Sergeant Stan Hollis[2] of the Green Howards, who did exactly that only a few hundred yards from Harry and his men. He ran forward firing his Sten at an embrasure then climbed onto the roof of a bunker and lobbed grenades into it. He captured thirty Germans and enabled the advance to continue.

Harry, meanwhile, was having some slightly more modest success.

> Fighting in these villages was a stop-start affair. We were moving up with the advance, and shooting any Germans foolish enough to show themselves, but once we reached the villages it was very different. Although we had trained for it, the reality simply wasn't like that. It was very difficult to determine where a German sniper was. Remember a lot of these men had fought in Russia and were very experienced, which none of us were. We began to suffer losses among our own snipers I think simply because we had so little combat experience. I recall two of us were trying to find a sniper we were told had hidden in the roof of a cottage, but there were several houses in front, all badly damaged and we couldn't spot him. There was quite a lot of pressure on us because the infantry had no armour and this man was holding us up. The next thing was my observer flew backwards with a shout. A bullet had hit his binoculars but ricocheted upwards. He was very shaken and developed a tremendous black eye, but I thought I saw the muzzle flash from inside a room. There was no way I could angle myself to fire a killing shot, though, so we got a Bren gunner up with us to rake the room. There was no further firing from there, although I never heard if they found the sniper afterwards.

Moving through the countryside once off the beaches meant adopting more specific tactics that enabled the snipers to work independently of the infantry companies, while still staying in touch to deal with immediate threats. Half of the snipers would be allocated to the advancing infantry companies; the others would work under the guidance of the Intelligence Officer, or even the Battalion CO. When heading into country that had not been cleared, Harry explained that:

> Near to any action, the marching columns ceased and we adopted what we termed 'aircraft columns' which meant single lines of infantry placed on each side of the road or street, ready to disperse into cover as aircraft or enemy infantry started their attack. Single columns in street fighting were essential as the right-hand line would watch the windows on the opposite side of the street, and vice-versa. But as snipers, we did not join in on these single lines, but operated from them as follow-up support. Although all battalion snipers were trained as scouts, we *never* acted as point-men or first soldier on patrol as that was not our task. Our scouting was only part of our triple role as scout–sniper–observers and our scouting was usually a part of our normal sniper patrols of a two-man team ... sometimes though as a lone sniper depending on the circumstances.
>
> Our sniper sections consisted of soldiers with the rank of private, or rifleman, fusilier etc., as the case might be, plus a couple of NCOs (sometimes a sergeant, more often a corporal). All shared in equal dangers and the extreme hazards of sniper patrols, the only difference being that the NCO in addition had responsibility for running the section, making sure the equipment was working perfectly and ensuring that in-section training was carried out as new techniques became applicable. The NCOs carried out as many, if not more patrols than other section members.

In Normandy the Germans called their snipers *Heckenschützen* ('hedgerow-shooters') and they were very well equipped, not only with Mauser Kar 98k rifles fitted with excellent quality optics but also with a range of camouflaged face masks, ponchos and jackets, something the British had not adopted even by the end of the war. An odd characteristic of the German snipers was the fact that their specially selected Mauser rifles were fitted with a quite bewildering range of different types of telescopic sight and mounts, an oddly

D-Day and Into the Bocage

wasteful policy that squandered Germany's limited war resources for little practical benefit. Britain and the Commonwealth used just one pattern of rifle and scope in Europe and this minimalist approach was logistically far more efficient to effect repair and replacement than the complicated and over-burdened German one.

Approaching the hedgerows required great care, as enemy soldiers could be dug in mere yards away, and would not be visible until they opened fire. Among their most effective weapons were MG 42 medium machine guns, which were universally (and incorrectly) referred to by the soldiers as 'Spandaus'.[3] Harry got to know and hate their sound, which he said was like the ripping of a huge sheet of calico, and during the initial stages of the landings the most frequent calls he and his colleagues got were to deal with hidden MG teams.

> A section of our line was held up by a couple of Spandaus and we were asked to deal with them, so another sniper and I decided the only way was to work round their flank. We didn't know, but expected that they might have a sniper or two to cover them, which was quite usual. I believe they had developed the tactic during the last war. The hedgerow was dense but unfortunately led away from them. They were slightly uphill so we had to crawl up a shallow ditch that had some scrubby bushes growing around it. It was very slow going, and it was wet so we were soon soaked through. We couldn't hold our rifles in front of us, so had to sling them [over the shoulder] which was not normal practice. It took for ever but we eventually managed to reach a thick clump of bushes, from where we watched very carefully through our binoculars. Because of the density of the foliage beyond, it could be an ideal spot for a hidden German sniper. You must remember that all the time, we expected to be shot at from the German line and our hearts were pounding so hard I'm surprised they couldn't hear us. From time to time the machine guns would open up, always short bursts to conserve ammunition.
>
> We moved forwards, but couldn't get too far as the hedge began to peter out, and it was fairly open ground

A rare picture of a known German sniper, Bruno Sutkus, wearing full camouflage. Sutkus had 209 verified kills and was typical of the tough Eastern Front veterans who fought in Normandy. He was unusually fortunate not to have been promptly executed when he was captured.

beyond. I could see the helmet of a German about 250 yards away, and my mate said the other gun was closer but slightly lower in a depression. We observed for quite a while, but could not see any sign of other Germans, so I said I'd take the furthest and we'd shoot on the count of three. My scope was zeroed at 300 yards, so I didn't need to adjust it much, and my mate clicked his down a tad. On three, we both fired at the heads of the gunners, then reloaded. One German half rose and turned toward us but I shot him. We immediately retreated and crawled back along the hedge, using the banking for cover. There were often infantry and snipers covering the machine-gun teams and just because we had not seen them, this did not mean they weren't there.

It fell eerily silent and we were in a quandary, for moving forwards to observe better was simply too dangerous. Besides, capturing the gun position was not our job, so we retraced our tracks and eventually got back to our lines, telling the officer that we believed the guns were dealt with. We got a terse 'Thanks chaps' and they moved off up the hill.

There was no respite for the snipers, however, and they were continually being called upon to clear a path for the advancing rifle companies. Harry was not destined to stay with the Green Howards for very long, though, barely more than a week. The Germans had had plenty of time to register the range of every village or landmark precisely for their artillery and mortars, and salvoes of shells would suddenly rain down on the British troops, often when they had stopped to rest for the night. In particular the six-barrelled Nebelwerfer 43 mortars, nicknamed 'Moaning Minnies', were much hated, as unlike the curving track of an artillery shell, which announced its arrival with a rising shriek, the Nebelwerfer bombs dropped almost vertically and silently, arriving only with a brief, rising moaning sound. This provided no time to take cover, and even if a slit trench was nearby, their vertical trajectory meant that any form of trench was of little use. One of these shells almost proved Harry's undoing, for as he stood in the square of a small village conferring with some of his section, a sudden shower of Minnies gave them no chance whatsoever to head for shelter. They exploded with lethal effect on the hard pavement, sending shards of sharp steel splinters and pieces of stone in all directions. There were several men killed and many wounded, including Harry.

> I received a head wound as a piece of mortar penetrated my helmet and stuck in my head, at the same time my top lip was torn open nearly to the nose, plus other blast injuries. I was not capable of standing and was taken by stretcher to the Casualty Clearing Station [CCS] then moved to a Royal Army Medical Corps [RAMC] tent near Bayeux where I received treatment, but was classified as 'walking wounded' so was not returned to the UK. Instead, after further treatment I was returned to the front line as our infantry losses were mounting.[4]

It was an experience that cemented his decision always to wear his helmet and never a soft cap, which would later on prove to be a very wise move. The splinters in his left eye had damaged the nerves and taken away some of his vision and this wound was subsequently to have longer-term implications. However, as he was right-eyed he said it did not affect his shooting and interfered little with day-to-day life. In later years his eyesight began to deteriorate quite markedly in both eyes. As a small compensation, he found he was entitled to his first wound stripe.

> A wound stripe was a tiny, gold coloured strip usually sewn onto your sleeve by a nurse, and was only applicable if the injury was treated at a CCS or RAMC hospital, and the paybook stamped and signed by an RAMC doctor. My AB64 [paybook] showed this ... but in fact, many soldiers didn't bother to wear wound stripes.

To his initial dismay, Harry was not returned to the Green Howards, but ordered to report to the Hallamshire Battalion of the York and Lancaster Regiment (or Yorks and Lancs), with whom he was to remain for the rest of his service. The Hallamshires had not landed on the first day of the invasion, but were part of the follow-up reinforcements on 10 June, part of 146th Infantry Brigade, and they were universally known as 'The Polar Bears' because the 49th West Riding Infantry Division wore a roaring polar bear motif as a shoulder insignia. This was introduced to mark the division's service in Iceland in 1940–42. Although Harry took a while to establish himself, his clinical proficiency as a sniper was soon recognised and he became an integral part of the sniping section with whom he developed a strong bond.

> When I joined them, the first question from the other men was 'Wha's tha' from lad?' When I said Manchester, the response was 'Aye, thet's reet good enough,' as no one was interested in my abilities, just that I was from the right part of England!
>
> It was difficult at first, as I knew no-one, but the sniper section were a good bunch and our very efficient officer, Lieutenant Phillip Young, was an enthusiast who really knew his job. I later got to know the battalion CO, Colonel T. Hart-Dyke quite well and he was a great supporter of 'his' snipers, whom he regarded as indispensable to the efficient working of the battalion.

Chapter 4

Driving Inland

Fontenay-le-Pesnel, 25 June

HARRY WAS NOT SURE EXACTLY what the date was when he joined the Hallamshires, but it was certainly around mid-June, as on the 25th he took part in an attack that was an integral part of the planned break-out from the Normandy bridgehead. These were early days, of course, and life was to become progressively more difficult for the sniper teams. Harry had joined the battalion at a time when it had halted for the simple reason that bad weather had prevented vital supplies of small-arms ammunition from being offloaded at the Mulberry Harbours. He did take part in some observation patrols around Audrieu, which had been captured, though he could remember nothing eventful about them other than finding one or two unoccupied German sniper's hides. Finally, with the much-needed ammunition arriving, they moved on to the next objective. Harry was able instantly to recall the name of the village, Fontenay-le-Pesnel.

> We had been told that the defending unit were the 26th Panzergrenadiers and they were expected to be a tough nut to crack. [The village] was sitting in very open farmland, not at all good country for us snipers, sloping ground and nowhere to hide. Our officer decided that there was no point in wasting us in open attack and we were to wait until the barrage began and move up with the rifle companies. It was a terrific barrage too, when it began.

Fortunately, the morning dawned wet and very misty, helping to obscure the Hallamshire advance, as they slowly fought their way into the village. Mostly this was close-range combat, the

Germans firing from houses then retreating when the British doggedly pushed forwards. The defenders had also laid down a heavy smoke-screen, which had the intended effect of confusing the advancing British; several infantry companies veered off course, losing track of the ground marker tapes that had been laid to help them. The attack was to have one minor historical outcome, in that the Hallamshires' 6-pounder anti-tank guns used a new type of ammunition, APDS,[1] for the first time. This special warhead could punch through any German armour and the gun destroyed the first Panther tank ever to be knocked out by the infantry.

In fact, Harry saw the result later:

> After the fighting, I went and looked at the Panther tank. It was huge but our 6-pounder had knocked two holes right through the side armour and it had burned out. I believe the gunner was awarded a medal for this. I thought how useful these A/T guns would be and decided when I had the time, I'd ask to go on a training course to learn how to fire one. I wanted to be able to deal with a tank if the gunners were knocked out so I asked to be sent on the A/T course and qualified as a gunner. In fact, I never had to use that particular skill, but it was good to know I had the ability if circumstances dictated it.[2]

The employment of these anti-tank guns, normally 6-pounders but also the bigger 17-pounders, at battalion level, had been an early innovation, but it proved an extremely practical one. Taking the guns into the line with the infantry enabled enemy armour to be dealt with immediately, rather than having to call on artillery behind the lines to try and register on them, impossible if they were moving fast. The guns could deal with bunkers or snipers hidden in high buildings, too, as they could also fire high explosive rounds. As they moved cautiously forwards, Harry caught up with a party from HQ, who were under heavy fire from a tank machine gun so he followed the officer and the rest of the riflemen who had moved off to work their way around the edge of the houses, but they were under observation.

I was with a forward rifle company, and their officer had just been killed by a sniper concealed in a house. I tried to see a way to get forward unseen but it meant crossing the road in full view of the whole street. We couldn't tell where the shot had come from and eventually some of the infantry and I worked round the side but it was slow work and the sniper had long gone by the time we got behind the buildings. I did manage to silence a Spandau that was firing from a hedge beyond the village and we could see Germans heading back up the slope to the big wood behind. Deeper into the countryside [the hedgerows] became much more dense, and were completely intertwined. Savage fighting was from field to field non-stop, day and night without pause, as the constant attacks and counter-attacks swung each way. Our daily losses were really grim and we used to take a daily roll-call as it grew dark to see how many were left. We had so many killed and wounded, plus missing whom we hoped were POWs.

Tessel Wood, 28 June

The 'big wood' Harry referred to was called Tessel and it proved to be a major obstacle for the Hallamshires. Attached to HQ Company, the snipers took part in the heavy fighting in and around the wood, where it was proving very hard to dislodge the well dug-in Germans from their pre-prepared defences. The advance was far slower than predicted and although the Hallamshires eventually fought their way into the southern and eastern edges of the wood, the battalion was to be stuck there for almost three weeks. It was a poignant place for Harry, as it was here on 28 June that his Sniping Officer Capt. P. M. Young[3] was killed. Harry and his section were advancing towards the western edge of the village, over open farmland and into heavy artillery fire. The snipers were forward of their infantry and had dug slit trenches to shelter in, whilst spotting for any targets when a salvo of shells roared overhead.

They went over us and landed a few hundred yards behind. Lt. [sic] Young who was resting in his slit trench was mortally wounded and died from his injuries. The salvo of shells also targeted exactly the Battalion HQ and wounded several others, including the Commanding Officer who caught some splinters too. It was later thought that the battalion radio had been spotted by a German observer. The early loss of Lt. Young meant that he was much missed as he had been a real enthusiast who had trained with the snipers and quickly proved himself in action.

The fighting see-sawed to-and-fro, with local objectives being fought over, captured and lost, but always with the single plan in mind of allowing the Allies to advance further inland and away from the beaches. There was little time for rest; the snipers bedded down anywhere that there was a lull in the fighting, and Harry even fell asleep one evening in a waterlogged slit trench, utterly oblivious to the cold water. They lived with constant physical and mental fatigue and mostly ate from their ration packs, as it was impossible for them to carry anything except their combat kit and iron rations. This usually meant eating the food cold as it was too dangerous to light fires. This poor diet was a problem for all of the snipers (remember, Harry was just 20) as young men at that age habitually require large amounts of calories daily, and in combat this was reckoned to be 4,000 or 5,000 calories per man – as a minimum. Iron rations did not provide this much, so in purely medical terms, they were unable to take in enough nourishment to generate sufficient body heat or body energy to match the physical effort expended. This fatigue was later on closely linked to the effects of combat stress. It meant that they were constantly hungry, tired and cold, and while hot food was considered a priority for all soldiers, and the cooks performed sterling service in ensuring the fighting companies were fed, daily life for a sniper was different.

> All those of us who were in that fighting recall the hunger, getting food to the rifle companies in the front line was hit-and-miss and for the snipers it didn't happen at all. We snipers took hardtack with us and I always had my two water bottles to keep me going but I could only get back to HQ in the dark usually, and before I could find anything to eat, I had to go through debriefing, weapon cleaning and if

> I were lucky maybe a couple of hours asleep in a slit trench. My memories of Normandy are deeply scarred. That is why I never went back for fifty years. You don't go to places that were nightmares.

Harry also recalled that one of the most wearying but overlooked discomforts of the fighting was:

> Mostly the sheer noise of battle in those hedgerows was blasting our eardrums and my left ear was perforated, yet the occasional lull was unnerving – the quietness was so fragile that we could hear rifle bolts being worked very near to us. With the use of survey maps I always tried to let our battalion Intelligence Officer know where I hoped to lay up, well camouflaged. The reason for this was for him to let our support tanks have an idea too, for all the time tanks of both sides would suddenly crash at speed through the hedgerow and their tracks went over the bodies of both living and dead. If they knew in advance a sniper was out front, they were more careful, at least that was the hope. We were surrounded by the dead who we couldn't move as it was too dangerous ... The stench was unforgettable. In the heat of summer the bodies started very swiftly to decay, most were bloated and took on a strange colouring ... This attracted great swarms of insects which feasted on them and on us too, which led to dysentery.

This was a continual problem for absolutely everyone and Harry suffered quite badly, needing treatment at a Regimental Aid Post on more than one occasion and hospitalisation once he returned to Britain after the war. It left him with, as he put it, 'a wobbly digestive system' for the rest of his life. As many of the German snipers were Eastern Front veterans they were particularly adept at fighting in urban areas, many having seen a great deal of combat through the rabbit-warrens of tunnels and piled debris in cities such as Leningrad, and flushing them out of the many tiny hamlets and villages the Allies encountered was slow and nerve-wracking. However, even the Germans were not immune to making mistakes. On fighting into a small French village near Bayeux, Harry was

Cleaning was a vital but wearying chore. This photo purports to show a sergeant cleaning the rifle of a sleeping sniper. Harry was unconvinced, saying, 'No sniper would ever allow another soldier to touch his rifle and besides, the sergeant was using a captured German aluminium chain pull-through, [which the British believed damaged the rifle bore].'

told by an infantry sergeant that his unit had taken casualties from a sniper hidden in one of a row of cottages. He entered the rear of a cottage across the road and worked his way into the attic, from where he watched with binoculars through some shattered roof tiles. He could see no sign of movement, and no shots were fired.

> I decided this was going to be a slow business, as the German was clearly no novice and was not going to give his position away easily. I watched until my eyes ached and had to take a break, although with no tanks, the infantry couldn't advance so it was up to me, but they were in the room below me and were happy enough to take a rest and brew up some tea. I do recall one offered me a dixie of hot sweet tea and it was like nectar, I was parched. Eventually I went back to observing, when a tiny movement caught my eye. A wooden shutter had been swinging in the wind, and I saw a set of white fingers against the dark paint. He was slowly moving it back against the wall so I raised my rifle and fired just to the left of the shutter and called to the infantry to go. There was a great commotion, as they raced out and flattened themselves under the window opposite. A couple of grenades went in, and they disappeared inside. My shot had killed him and they brought out his scoped Mauser rifle, from which I took the telescopic sight, which I still have. If he had bothered to blacken his fingers, I doubt I would have seen the movement.

It was not only enemy small-arms fire that caused heavy casualties amongst the Hallamshires, but also 'friendly fire'.

> Friendly fire was all too common, and while the support 25-pounders usually sent their shelling over us, none of us could say the same for the bigger guns firing from near the beaches as we constantly had 'shorts' fall around us so casualties were inevitable. Mortaring was intense and blasting all hedges with machine-gun fire was the rule, so typically the lifetime of a sniper, on either side, was short.

Harry said of one example of the fighting in the region (likely at Tessel) that it was:

eant H. M Furness, aged
photographed in May 1945,
after the war ended. The
age to his left eye from
mortar splinters is clear, as
s apparent pleasure at no
er being a target for enemy
ers.

only family photograph
Harry's daughter could
, taken just before the
reak of the war. From left:
her John, mother Jesse,
in Jean, Harry ('Kid')
ess and Harry junior. He
tated the rear: 'I carried
photo with me as I waded
e ... on D-Day. Damage
ed during action and
ess, even though protected
st sea water at the time.'

One of Harry's instructors, Captain Underhill (universa known by all as 'Uncle') lecturing to a group of neop Scottish snipers. Notice the all wearing Denison smocks have Scout telescopes slung their shoulders.

A sniper in training, he is wearing a Patt. 1943 Windp Smock. These, with matchi trousers, were issued to be over the top of the battledre The drawstrings of the hoo can be seen on his shoulder His steel helmet is heavily camouflaged with scrim and hessian strips as is his rifle, Aldis-scoped P. 14 Mk I W indicating this is perhaps a early photograph.

ne image of a pair of Canadian snipers in full ghillie suits. The left sniper has moved his large
t pouches almost underarm, to enable him to lie down comfortably. Behind him is a wire hide
e type mentioned by Harry. When properly covered in foliage it would have been an excellent
place from which to snipe.

eadly combination of a
an machine-gun crew and
 watching for approaching
y units. Although taken
ssia in 1943, this publicity
 demonstrates well the
y effective type of defensive
 the Allies faced in their
ce through North-West
e.

Top: Canadians landing on Juno Beach on D-Day. The small size of the 'Landing Craft, Assau[lt]' apparent and the soldiers are all wearing newly issued Patt. 1944 'turtle' helmets.

Above: An aerial view of *bocage* country; every hedgerow could be defended by concealed snip[ers,] infantry or machine guns and the near-impenetrable growth made it, as Harry said 'a nightm[are'.]

sh Commandos advance
d Sherman tank cover,
g just landed on Sword
 on D-Day. This is exactly
rea in which Harry had his
combat experience.

of the many innovations
g the invasion was the
thrower tank, in this
ce a Churchill Mk VII
odile' showing the
tating blast of flame from
essurised projector.

of the most feared of all
an infantry weapons,
IG 42 machine gun.
d by crews of three, these
ositioned to provide
ocking fields of fire
g an impassable killing
 In this case the crew
llschirmjager (Luftwaffe
ute troops) photographed
g the defence of Arnhem.

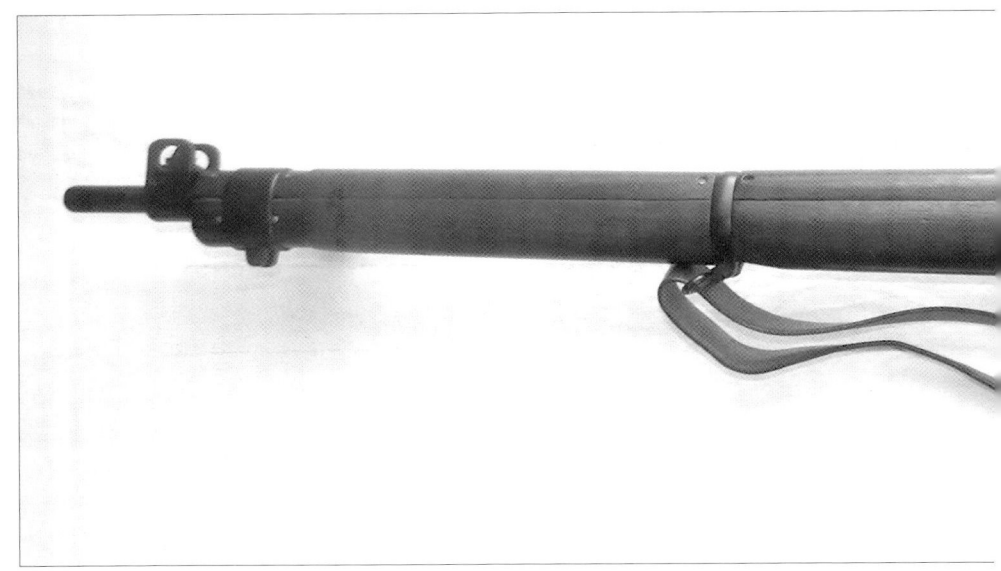

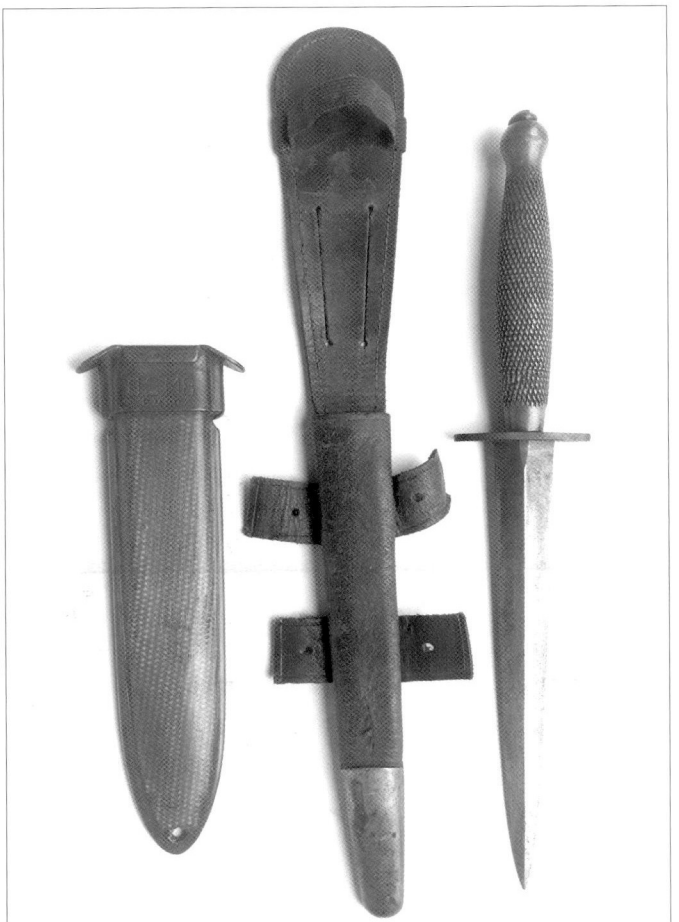

The 2nd Pattern Fairbairn-Sykes knife carried by Har[ry] during the campaign in North-West Europe. The b[lade] shows considerable use and he swapped the fragile leat[her] issue sheath for an Americ[an] M3 knife-bayonet scabbar[d which] held the blade more secure[ly] using internal spring clips.

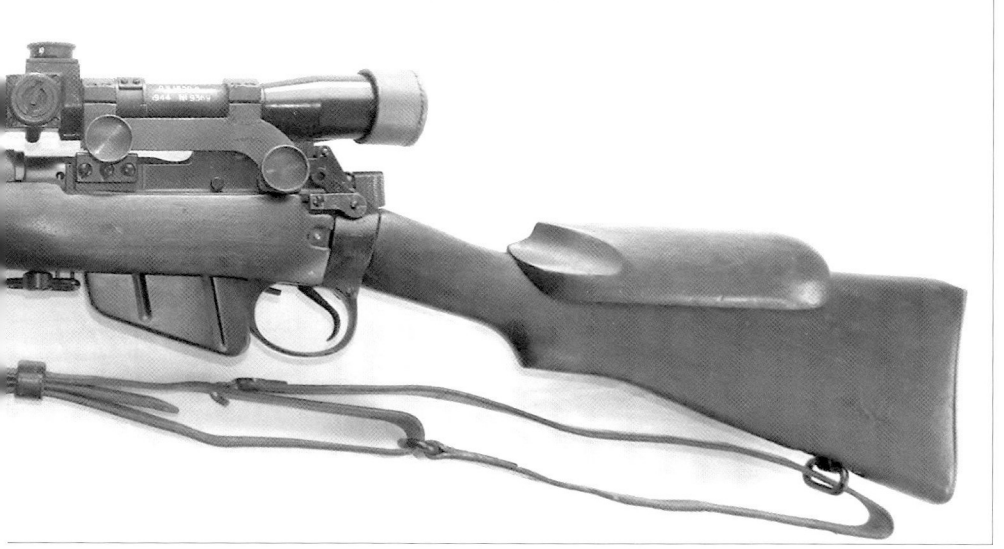

Harry's 'No. 2 rifle', left side, used as his back-up during the campaign. It is in standard configuration, with its Mk II scope and all matching numbers. Alas, its total refurbishment at Warminster in the mid-1980s removed its patina of use, something Harry always regretted.

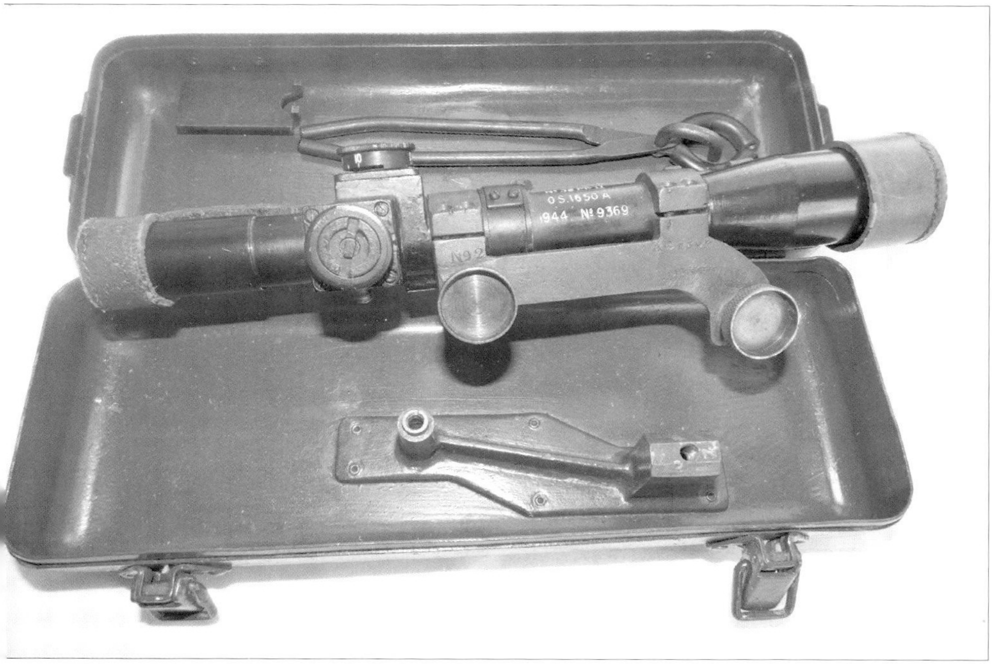

Harry's 'Case, Tel. No. 8 1941'. This is a very early example and it retains the small spring-clamp in the lid that originally held the first pattern rotating-drum-type adjuster tool. The two solid threaded brass posts into which the telescope is screwed are visible. In the lid are the later issue tongs and adjuster to enable the turrets to be re-set after zeroing.

An infantry platoon of the Hallamshires in 'aircraft column' advancing through Normandy, July 1944. The snipers are out of sight and would be ahead of the column, ensuring there were no unpleasant surprises.

A US Sherman 'Rhino' hedge cutter in Caen. Developed to deal with the *bocage* by the simple expedient of welding blades on the front to burst through hedges, one can see why Harry and his fellow snipers were terrified of finding themselves in the path of one

A sniper-scouting patrol in the *bocage*. This gives a good idea of how dense the foliage was, although Harry questioned the suggestion that snipers ever patrolled like this. Nevertheless, close inspection of the image shows that the two soldiers are snipers. They wear no insignia and are both carrying scopeless No. 4 (T) rifles which appear to have camouflage paint on them. Some infantry units did use snipers in this manner.

od image of a working
er, Private James Donald
e King's Own Scottish
lerers, in Holland, late
. His visible fatigue and
-spattered rifle show he is
much engaged in 'active
ce', though Harry would
disapproved very strongly
s cigarette!

One of the Hallamshires' 6-pounder anti-tank guns of the type Harry trained on. This AFPU image was taken in Willemstad, Holland, 8 November 1944. The transfer of these guns from Royal Artillery to infantry command was a stroke of tactical brilliance and materially helped the Allies break through the German defences.

A Kangaroo troop carrier, ba on a Sherman chassis. They saved hundreds of lives as th soldiers sheltering within we immune to small-arms fire and anti-personnel mines. A direct hit from a mortar w dangerous, but the Kangaro speed made this a very rare occurrence.

A Nebelwerfer 41 being reloaded. Much feared by the allies, it could fire a salvo of six 158 mm 2-inch) HE rockets each with a payload of 6 lb of TNT out to 4.3 miles. The size of the projectile is clear from the soldier carrying one. Harry was wounded twice by Nebelwerfer fire.

An excellent image of a working Black Watch sniper in a roof hide in Gennep, Holland. If it is a genuine combat image, then clearly he was not too concerned about enemy sniper activity, as normally he would never sit in plain sight.

Nijmegen Bridge photographed as allied troops cross it shortly after its capture. This was a pivotal part of the success of the campaign in Holland. Two dead Germans still lie in the foreground and others near the left bridge support.

Buffalo amphibious vehicles off-loading their cargo of Bren Gun Carriers near the IJssel River in Holland. The Buffalo in the foreground has a pair of .50-calibre Browning machine guns behind steel shields, providing some potent firepower.

hastily posed press photo of a British sniper in a snowsuit. His magazine is barely retained in the rifle, which is obviously un-camouflaged, and he wears no gloves. The reason for the 'dark splodges' that Harry mentioned painting on his kit can be understood when looking at the foliage behind this man.

A Churchill Crab flail tank in the centre of Arnhem, 15 April 1944. The chains were sacrificial, one usually being blown off each time the flail struck a mine, but the crew could easily replace them from spares carried. Their introduction literally helped to pave the way for the Allied advance.

Taken during the shooting championships at Haltern, Harry poses with his No. 4 (T) rifle.

One of the first photos Harry took of Erni looking as she did on the day he first saw he

Harry standing on the spot in Berlin where Hitler's body had been burned. He was with his Battalion Intelligence Officer, and a drunk Russian soldier threatened to shoot them.

Harry and Erni's wedding day. He wears th uniform pictured on page 143. Harry said th Erni wore a Chanel suit that she particular treasured because she had so few clothes.

[pi]cture taken in the late 1970s, Harry holding [N]ikon F, with a Leica slung around his neck. [O]n his wrist is his venerable Omega sniper's [wa]tch, which he wore for almost thirty years. [U]nusually he has long hair, due to constant travel for work.

Harry and his brother John, in his Royal Signals uniform. Harry thought this was taken just after John returned home for demobilisation. Annette said her uncle did not recover mentally from the wounds he sustained, never married and became reclusive as he grew older.

[Ha]rry and Erni celebrate their 70th wedding anniversary.

Their final resting place. Theirs was indeed a true WWII love story.

Harry holding his 'No. 2' sniping rifle photographed at his home in 2004.

Unremitting and horrendous. We lived on our nerves and there were so many incidents that after a while they all seemed to merge into one. I can't now recall much of what I did, other than an overwhelming feeling of tension the whole time. We had no proper rest, there was always something to be dealt with. I had several very close calls with German snipers, though I don't recall where or when. There were no days, as such, just dawns and dusks, when we went out. I recall sleeping in a slit trench and being shaken by someone who was trying to wake me, but I felt as though I was drugged.

The only incident I do remember was having to track down a German sniper who had killed an officer and several riflemen. The advance round the wood had stopped, but no one could locate him. [Our infantry] were in the wood as well, so artillery was out of the question. My officer asked me to go up with another sniper to deal with the problem. The infantry sergeant told us all of the shots were in their heads and the men were too afraid to try and advance as he never seemed to miss.

It was terrible ground to search, as it had fallen trees and churned-up undergrowth, and you could be ten feet from the sniper and not see him. The only way was to try and draw his fire, so my chum and I crawled very carefully forward. He lay behind a fallen trunk and gently shook a branch with a stick while I was watching through my binoculars. But nothing happened. We had to be so careful as it might become obvious we were trying to trap him. My chum took off his helmet and he very, very, slowly moved it along, on his stick just behind the trunk, and a shot was fired. I didn't see the flash but there was a definite shaking from a small patch of foliage where several branches had fallen down. He was very close, I thought about 150 yards, so we conferred in whispers and each moved to the opposite ends of the tree. I had the root system in front of me, which was ideal, and my chum had a lot of foliage. I fired first, then he followed, and we each put, I think, three rounds into the area where he was. We tried the helmet trick again, raising it infinitely slowly but there was no response.

We crawled back and reported that we believed we had dealt with him and took a sergeant and Bren gunner back to the tree, to show where he was. They put a lot of fire into the area and then our riflemen moved up. We did hear later that he was found with two fatal bullet wounds, so I assume we did our job properly. More often, though, we never did hear if our efforts had been successful.

It was at this stage that they finally began to advance beyond the dreaded *bocage* country, to the huge relief of the snipers and just about everyone else.

We had finally completely left that hell on earth, the *bocage* country. The ground opened out with more fields and smaller woods. Of course, the Germans knew the countryside well, and were becoming far more organised as the fighting progressed. In particular they began laying booby-traps for us as they had more time to prepare positions and plan fighting retreats, which they were very good at doing. I had heard they had booby-trapped the dead, ours and theirs, in the *bocage* so that follow-up troops would be killed when they went to bury them. I never personally experienced this, but ordinary booby-traps were in constant use by the German Army nevertheless, so we had to be careful to avoid them.

Common uses were grenades or other explosives connected to lavatory pulls, doors, water-wells, boxes of all sorts, especially if they looked to hold wine or … any items of use left in wrecked houses. In particular we were plagued with mines of many types but the little anti-personnel box mines and 'S' or 'Schu' mines,[4] which we called 'Bouncing Bettys' or 'De-bollickers' took a heavy toll on fast advancing infantry. The 'S' mines had three very short spikes sticking out of the ground which were usually hidden by grass … they exploded if you brushed against the spikes. The box mines were difficult to spot in advance as they were dug in just a few inches and lightly covered with soil or grass cuttings, etc. They looked like a very small mound, and once you stepped or crawled on it, then you could hear the box snap shut and any slight pressure or movement exploded it. It was possible to move over the anti-tank mines, which were the size of a large dinner plate, often just hidden under a thin layer of soil and if you were looking intently, they could be spotted in time. Our BGCs [Bren Gun Carriers][5] and Jeeps had layers of packed sandbags on the floors to lessen the blast but for the infantry and us, it was a slow, painstaking business as minefields were so wide that even the snipers carried knives for prodding the ground if we ever found ourselves trapped in a minefield.

Further hazards, particularly nearer to enemy lines, were trip wires, often just tin cans with pebbles in them that jangled if you brushed against them but they could at times be pre-primed with grenades. Even the slightest movement would pull out the retaining pins and explode the grenade in a few seconds. Any explosion would immediately bring retribution in the form of most intense machine-gun and mortar fire so we were very careful not to set one off.

We became so tired that it was possible to fall asleep the moment we stopped moving, so trying to sit in a slit trench or hide, and then concentrate, was next to impossible. One of us would watch, the other have forty winks, then we'd swop over. We couldn't have worked otherwise. Fighting like that in an assault was too intense and fast to really remember anything now, although one of our snipers was killed, which was a loss we all felt keenly. We were very tight-knit and by then we all knew each other's capabilities and could rely utterly on each other.

We advanced again and I recall it was almost a repetition of the previous fight, with heavy resistance from Germans on a hill overlooking the river. We targeted the machine gunners, who were the greatest threat, but it was difficult as we couldn't get close enough to ensure killing shots. We were able to fire suitably close to make them keep their heads down, and luckily a squadron of tanks had arrived, who crushed the opposition very comprehensively. What I do remember is the luxury of being put on lorries to be taken forwards!

Vendes, 16 July

As the British forces advanced deeper inland, the requirement to keep up the momentum of the advance became more imperative, the fighting never letting up for a minute. This part of the campaign was the well-planned and crucial break-out from the Normandy bridgehead and XXX Corps, including the Hallamshires and King's Own Yorkshire Light Infantry (KOYLI), were ordered to attack Barbe Farm, just south of Tessel Wood, with the objective of securing the town of Vendes beyond it. The fighting for the farm became desperate, often hand-to-hand, and at one point two companies of the Hallamshires were surrounded.

> This wood was dense and had been heavily shelled, but was useful as we were well placed a little above and behind the farm and were kept busy with no lack of targets. In particular we tried to silence any machine guns, which we managed, I believe, with some success. I shot two Germans at the same gun, one having replaced the first, and I fired several times at the gun itself to try and render it u/s [unserviceable] although I have no idea if I did so. The infantry at times actually closed with the Germans hand-to-hand.
>
> The one other incident I do recall was that the infantry were held up by accurate fire from the church tower. It was not a place that we would have chosen for sniping, but this German was certainly dedicated. Two of us went up to see what we could do, but there was no obvious target for us, and it was also very high, so difficult to shoot upwards into. Our bullets would have been hitting the ceiling inside. Eventually, the officer called for an artillery strike on the church, which soon settled the matter.
>
> Finally the CO ordered a retreat from the farm and our battalion laid down a heavy barrage of mortars and Vickers fire and I think also some heavy artillery. I was with another sniper, and we stayed behind to provide covering fire. Specifically, the open ground could have enabled one German machine gun to have cut down all of the retiring men, so we made sure they did not get a chance.

> We were astonished in the middle of it all to see one of our ambulances driving up almost to the farm to collect wounded.[6] Eventually, we returned accompanied by our Major (Londsdale-Cooper) who had helped load on the wounded and I think we were the last ones back.

Although the attack failed to secure Barbe Farm, it did achieve its overall objective in tying up German forces and causing other reserves to be drafted in to help replace losses. Harry was oblivious to the greater plan being, as he put it, 'completely washed-out' and the battalion was put into rest, which as he said was a great relief to all concerned. All of the men were utterly exhausted and the fighting was becoming progressively harder as more German reinforcements arrived. Fatigue makes men dull-witted, their reaction times are slower and mistakes happen, but it was worse for the snipers, who not only went forwards with the infantry during the day, but regardless of their physical state, often had to go out in the evenings to gather intelligence on enemy positions. Harry said as an aside that two hours' unbroken sleep a night for snipers was normal, sometimes he managed just by having cat-naps. When they went on night patrols, the snipers were always in pairs to watch out for each other. There were also other, unwelcome hazards.

> The average infantryman becomes very trigger-happy and will shoot at anything to be on the safe side to protect his own life. I can best illustrate that from an incident which happened to me on return from a lone sniper patrol. If possible, we tried to keep the same snipers with one company so they would get used to each other's routines. Also, as a precautionary technique against being spotted, we made it a general rule to leave our lines for our sniper patrols by going out via one company position and returning via another company's position as an alternate route back to HQ. This was to prevent an ambush by patrolling Germans who might be following a sniper's routine. As we left before sunrise and returned after dark, we had to be very careful to let our forward patrols know when to expect us coming in. So, we also … had a password to call out when we got near company OPs. This

particular night I was coming in after a very long day and I was exhausted and in no mood for the very nervous Bren gunner, who kept firing bursts towards me as I lay flat on the ground shouting out the password. Although not given to using bad language usually, I was swearing at him like a trooper to stop shooting. Luckily an NCO recognised my voice just before the entire line opened up, it needed only a grenade or two to be thrown and I would have 'bought it' as we used to say. Lack of communication in the forward areas is called 'the fog of war'.

Because of the infantrymen's general lack of understanding about the role of snipers, they were often the butt of derogatory comments, particularly as Harry and his section inevitably had to pass through their forward lines to go on patrol. They would hear muttered imprecations of 'the killers are out again' or 'make way for the murder patrol', which didn't endear the infantry to him. On one occasion he became so cross at the attitude of the men whose lives he was trying so hard to protect, that in no-man's land he used his knife to cut open a very dead and gas-inflated cow which poisoned the entire area with its foul smell. It was a small act of protest that he said, with a wry smile, satisfied him tremendously and made him feel a little better about men who appeared so ungrateful at times. There was also the fact that the presence of a British sniper in a sector of line would often result in harsh retaliation on the part of the Germans. The battalion riflemen understandably resented being left to face heavy mortar or machine-gun fire once the sniper had completed his work and slipped away.

Harry did stress that the snipers were never in open conflict with their infantry, it was more a case of his colleagues not comprehending what was actually involved and rarely seeing the end result. This was the downside to being one of such an elite band. Aside from working in secrecy most of the time, they had little time for social contact with other soldiers, working dawn to dusk and often patrolling at night. The ordinary soldiers regarded their nocturnal prowling as an irritation as they had to be constantly vigilant in case the figure emerging silently from the gloom was a foe, not friend.

Naturally, enemy soldiers were even less tolerant, British snipers were warned by instructors that surrender was seldom an option if caught and capture simply meant a bullet in the head followed, if anyone could be bothered, by a cursory burial in the nearest slit trench. After the war many captured German snipers were tried as 'war criminals' by the Soviet authorities, a somewhat hypocritical attitude in view of the number of Russian snipers employed.

About this time, Harry was having some trouble with his rifle, as the scope would not hold zero. There was no immediate repair available so it had to be returned to the REME workshops, who were following up. Harry, mindful of his reliance on his Enfield, had already made plans for such an eventuality, as previously described, and his spare No. 4 (T) was soon put to good use.

> I had my number two rifle back at battalion HQ, with the kit I didn't need, so when I was given permission to return to hand my rifle in for repair, I unpacked it and brought it back with me. I was a very highly trained sniper and not about to sit out the fighting with no rifle, but the only problem was that the new rifle had been zeroed a long while before and I was now using a totally different batch of ammunition, so it required re-zeroing.[7] The front line is not the place to do this and I was not going into action until it was satisfactorily zeroed. I found a quiet spot near an old quarry, paced out 100 and 300 yards and began to zero it using a homemade target. One of my mates came with me to spot for me and he called corrections as I fired. It did not take long. I think that the ammunition was very similar [to that previously used] and I was happy that it was deadly accurate at 300 yards. It also had a Mk II scope on it, which I thought better than my Mk I.

The battalion had been in continuous action for thirty-three days and it was withdrawn for a week to the small village of Ducy Ste-Marguerite near Bayeux. As usual coming out of action never really provided a proper chance of rest for the snipers. Rifles and spotting equipment had to be meticulously cleaned, and the men had to make reports on their actions and intelligence observations.

> When we came out of the line, we snipers had a debrief with the IO when we discussed any problems that we had had, or experiences that we thought might be of help to others in the section. The new problem was that [sniper] casualty rates were so high that we were now short-handed, as replacements were not coming through fast enough to make up the losses. I mentioned before that all of us were volunteers ... nobody was just ordered to become a sniper simply because he was a good shot, and we were known to try and recruit the occasional marksman we knew of in the rifle companies. If they showed interest then we'd take them out to try out as a second in a team of two; we'd train them 'in-section' so-to-speak, but we very quickly returned them to their company if they were unsuitable, as simply being a good shot was insufficient for doing our kind of task. They at least had combat experience by then, so were not completely 'green'.

As the war had moved from the beachhead inland, a school was established near Audrieu, to speed up the training of snipers. Eventually there were three schools, although details of their exact whereabouts are now hard to determine. Harry had received his repaired rifle by this time, and was able to zero it, using a new batch of heavy ball cartridges that he had tucked away after begging them from the Kensingtons' Vickers teams.

> One of the snipers had found a good spot with a bit of a chalk quarry on level ground, and we paced out 300 yards. We then spent some time making sure our rifles were working properly and deadly accurate. My scope had been replaced with a Mk II and it was excellent. I'm not sure now, but I think the pads had been renewed as well and they had been centre-punched to stop them undoing which was standard practice on all of our sniping rifles by then.

There was no let-up for the sniper section, who had to carry out continual patrols and intelligence gathering. It did at least enable Harry to catch up a little on sleep, as well as having the luxury of both hot water and hot food.

It wasn't a rest by any means but we did manage to replace lost items of kit, I managed to find another pair of field-glasses, German ones that I swapped with one of our infantrymen. They were excellent, Zeiss, and I used them for the rest of the war. We did hear that our popular CSM[8] had been killed by mortars, which saddened us all. There was not a great amount of German resistance here but we had to patrol in case of counter-attack or raids and we had the joy of being able to wash clothes, which we hadn't done since we landed, so you can imagine the state they were in. Most of us snipers were unshaven, partly deliberate to keep our faces darker and taking those beards off was a painful experience.

It was at this stage that Harry had an experience that was to test his sniping skills to the utmost, when he was spotted by a German sniper.

We were at a small town, on its outskirts, and the rifle companies were gradually clearing it. I had found a damaged house and installed myself upstairs, lying prone as a shell had torn a large hole in the brickwork near the floor. I had a good view down the street and was looking through my scope for any sign of German activity. A bullet suddenly tore through the hole, blasting brick dust into my face and cutting me slightly. Luckily, I was lying at a slight angle as we never faced straight out of a hide to shoot, for I would have been killed had I not done so. This shook me as I could not understand how I could have been spotted and I wriggled well back into the room, wiped my face and knelt just high enough to see out of a corner of the window. I was camouflaged up so I knew my face was not visible, but a second shot came through the window, about two feet from me. I decided that, somehow, I was under observation, and took to the stairs, leaving by the back door and moving several houses up the road. A very badly hit house with a lot of the roof collapsed provided me with a good hide, and I very slowly moved upstairs.

I hoped the sniper might have thought I had been hit, and I used my binoculars balanced on a big roof timber to spot for him. I could see nothing that might give him away and watched as the infantry moved very cautiously up the street. There was a shot and one of the riflemen slumped down. He remained partly upright I remember, as he was against a wall. Everyone scattered, and a Bren gunner opened up on a house across the road. He absolutely peppered it with bullets and the brickwork looked like it was on fire with dust and sparks. If I was the sniper there, I would have moved places pretty smartly, as at that range .303 bullets would punch right through two courses of bricks. There were two houses next door very badly damaged with the roofs down but on the other side one had apparently escaped any damage at all.

I heard someone downstairs calling quietly, and it was one of our sniper section asking if I had pinpointed the German. He came up and I told him I reckoned that he would have moved to the undamaged house. We both watched but could see nothing, then had a stroke of luck. The rifle company had called up a BGC which arrived and stopped at the street corner, the Vickers gun in it raking the houses, and we both saw a tell-tale flash from inside the upper room of a house. The BGC reversed quickly, though I never knew if anyone had been hit. We knew he was there but couldn't see him, so had a quick conflab about where we thought he would be, which was at the bottom left of the window, so he could use the wall to protect his body as he fired. It was less than 300 yards away and we both fired, I slightly higher than my mate and we repeated our shots having varied our point of aim a little. My mate ran back downstairs to ask the Bren gunner to keep up covering fire on the room and the riflemen crept along the frontage. Two then slung No. 36s [Mills grenades] through the upper window, and they rushed in. I recall one grenade bounced out again and wounded some of our own soldiers. Eventually they emerged, one of them holding a very nice, brand-new German Mauser G43 semi-automatic sniping rifle. We had not come across one of these before, so said we'd take it back for our IO to see, which we did. I believe he sent it back to HQ to be tested and examined.

Beyond the *Bocage*: Caen, July–August

Finally, the Allied battle plan was beginning to prove its worth, and on 25 July the American forces were able to break out of the Cherbourg peninsula, advancing almost unchecked for the next ten days. They caught up with the German forces near Falaise, forcing them into a narrow pocket through which they had to retreat in full view of the merciless 1st Polish Armoured Division, who wreaked a terrible revenge on the densely packed, slowly moving German columns. Constant Allied air attacks doubled the misery for the Germans. A veteran Typhoon pilot and friend of the author said that as he approached the huge column of smoke at 5,000 feet above Falaise, he would shut his cockpit hood and use oxygen to try and keep the smell of the burning flesh out of his nose. The total of German casualties has never been truly established; some 50,000 surrendered but total losses killed, wounded and missing have been put as high as 200,000.

The developing war of pursuit as the German front crumbled was a novelty to the snipers, who often found themselves being moved up in Bren Gun Carriers to what was loosely defined as the front line. This was eminently practical, for they frequently worked alongside the reconnaissance units; the snipers not only provided cover for them, but were also able to observe and make their own notes from their advanced positions.

> We were very useful to the reconnaissance platoon as we had our Scout Telescopes and could observe what type of units the Germans belonged to. Indeed, we were able to determine sometimes the exact regiments in front of us. We observed build-ups of armour, artillery and the siting of mortar pits as well as ammunition dumps. All of this we recorded carefully and reported back to our IO. It was a treat to travel in the Bren Carriers as they simply flew along. Though we were bounced up and down like sacks of potatoes it was a huge improvement over footslogging.

Around this time, Harry recalled an instance when his normal caution was over-ridden and he nearly became another battlefield statistic. He was due to go on a patrol but was a little late starting off, and as he recounted:

> The list of places to avoid was a long one: church or bell towers, any trees, lonely bushes, ridges without cover, haystacks, being too near a window or an aperture from which your rifle barrel or muzzle blast, barrel pluming [smoke], reflections from telescopic sights, binoculars, telescope etc., etc. … For some reason now long forgotten I left our forward lines far too late; it was already starting to get light for we always made sure we left our positions in darkness to ensure we had time to find a good hide and wouldn't be spotted as we made our way into the unknown areas of no-man's land. On this occasion I just couldn't find a suitable place to lie up all day to carry out effective sniping. The area was fairly barren. A farmhouse I looked over seemed to be too isolated and left me with no escape exit once I started to shoot from it.
>
> No place seemed good enough to me; finally all that was left was a haystack within an open framework under a tin roof. I didn't like the idea at all, but as it was now quite light, I needed a place fast and thought that at least I could use it for observation purposes. I started to pull out hay so that I could pull myself up and slide feet-first inside the stack and then pull hay in front of me; I had already started to slide into the hay when suddenly I actually felt the passage of bullets as they smacked into the stack right next to me … I reacted within a fraction of a second and threw myself out of the stack, still holding my 4T rifle. I landed in a heap on the ground as another burst of fire hit the stack above me. I knew it was a Spandau from the very fast rate of fire, being shot in small bursts for accuracy. It all happened so fast I hardly recall how I managed it, but I was up and dashed past the haystack and found only a high hedge in front of me with no other place to go, as the MG kept firing bursts, I threw myself right over the top of the high hedge. I'm sure now, that if it had been a sports event it would have been

a record running high-jump, but as I hit the ground on the other side of that hedge I was still holding my rifle. And I got away as fast as I could from that MG.

Only after I had put some distance behind me, I realised I was walking in a peculiar way and then found that one of my boot heels had been completely shot-away, so that MG nearly got me … I suppose that in his excitement at having flushed out a Tommy sniper, his aim had let him down. When I got back to the battalion, they all had a good laugh at my expense and I remember that as I walked about some of the lads at HQ whistled that familiar Laurel and Hardy tune. I had to walk like that until I could get a pair of new boots. But I never went near a haystack again after that very close call.

After the scare of this narrow escape, he was to have another unwanted thrill when out on an early patrol with another sniper:

It was very early a.m. and barely light as two of us from the sniper section came out of the orchard and onto a small, heavily cambered roadway. We were on our way forward to find a suitable position amongst the hedgerows from where we could operate that day. We both kept right into the ditch as we went along, when we heard the sound of a fast-approaching motorcycle, but couldn't see it as the roadway in front curved away from us. We knew it couldn't be one of our DRs as our battalion wasn't so far advanced. My mate ran across to the opposite side of the road and lay in the ditch as I too got down. As soon as the German despatch rider appeared round the curve I fired immediately and he spun off his bike and fell back into the roadway, and his motorcycle continued into the ditch. I rushed towards the German soldier who was wearing a helmet with goggles and a long waterproof coat. It was very obvious to both of us that we would have to be very fast in taking anything off him useful for our Intelligence Officer, for the sound of the shot would alert any other German soldiers in that area. My mate was up and got to him very quickly; he removed from the DR's belt a small pistol and holster, I just had time to take the map-case which had been slung around his shoulders, then we moved away quickly. As it happened, each of us thought we had been the only one to shoot, but in fact we had both fired at precisely the same fraction in time as the two bullet wounds in his chest could clearly be seen. I was rather disappointed at not having got the pistol first, for when I got the chance to look at it properly, I recall it was not a proper military type at all, but a very nice civilian 7.65 mm calibre with two magazines inside a soft leather holster. Altogether rather unusual and as I had always liked handguns, I would have liked it. As for the map case I know it went back to Intelligence but never did hear if it had anything of importance in it.

It is most unusual for a sniper to get the opportunity to bring down an enemy despatch rider but this particular mission was very unusual in another way, for snipers are taught in Sniper School *never* to approach or deal with enemies shot down; it is exceedingly risky to do so. If ever caught next to a dead enemy for whom you are responsible it is certain to be your own end too as you will be shot on the spot. Yet in this instance both of us took the extraordinary risk as it was obvious a DR would be carrying both maps and despatches useful to our Intelligence Officer.

There was a postscript to this tale, which Harry later recounted.

It was very soon afterwards, perhaps a couple of days, when the sniper I had been out with on that occasion was severely wounded (and died later, I heard). He had been with a forward platoon which came under heavy mortar attack. A private in the platoon ended up with that pistol and even though his pals told him to get rid of it after having had two owners already, he refused but soon he too was killed. By then the story of that jinxed pistol got around and nobody wanted it, but as soon as I heard it was available, I went over and got it and paid no attention to the advice everyone gave to leave it alone. So, in a short period it had three owners, but I survived. Some time later I sold it to an American GI from an airborne unit who had come around to ask if we had any captured pistols to sell to our GI buddies. Many years later I happened to see a War Office photograph ... which showed a flattened German soldier who had been run over by tank tracks and in the ditch was a motorcycle. I wasn't pleased to see it, but it seemed familiar, though I cannot say if it was related to the same incident.

The Hallamshires in fact halted at Poussy-la-Campagne on 16 August, which was south and slightly east of Caen. They were to wait for more reinforcements to move up before continuing the advance east towards the city of Lisieux. Such short respites allowed the usual much-needed catch-up of sleep, but also briefings for the sniper teams on the new ground situation. Working ahead of their own advanced lines, the snipers needed to gather as much geographical information as possible, not only to report to their Intelligence officers, but also to ensure the advancing riflemen did not fall into German ambushes. Of course, it was as much for their own benefit as well, to ensure they did not walk into enemy-held territory through lack of local knowledge.

During this period, although he was not certain of the date, Harry nearly lost his life because of a target that he believed was too good to pass up. This account is reproduced in full.

> It happened just as we were breaking out of the Normandy bridgehead. The CO sent me forward to report back any enemy movement and see if I could spot any artillery or dug-in tanks in advance of a battalion-strength attack. The situation in front was unclear and I left our forward companies in their slit trenches crawling very carefully to find a good concealed position ahead of our lines. I was using my 22× telescope to get the best possible view of where the German soldiers were likely to be concentrated. Soon, I saw something very interesting, a group of the enemy were partly hidden behind a hedgerow and trees. They were obviously officers, so they were priority targets. As I watched them through my high-powered scope, I could see quite clearly that the officer in the centre of the group was receiving deferential treatment from all the

others as they looked at him as they were looking at our positions through their field glasses.

To spot such an inviting group was an opportunity I simply couldn't pass up and I needed to be fast. I put my scope down and picked up my rifle, as I was already lying prone. I just needed to estimate the range which I judged to be about 600 yards. Fortunately, I had already loaded some long-range heavy ball ammunition that I had managed to cadge from the 2nd Kensingtons' Vickers section. Previously I had zeroed my rifle for this type of ammunition. So, I was confident that when I fired, I had secured a good solid hit as the officer in the centre dropped. I knew that he must have had a high rank but was too far away to be able to identify any insignia.

As I fired, I lost my sight picture through the recoil but by the time I regained it he was down and the officers around him were in uproar, I could see them pointing in my general direction and I knew they must have seen my muzzle flash as most of them were watching our front lines, and I was concealed directly in their line of sight.

I immediately started to crawl away, not stopping to shoot at any other officers, as I knew I had to get away fast but the sheer speed of their retaliation was staggering. It appeared to be immediate, as they probably had fire orders from their officers. Their aim was excellent and all around me were explosions from shellfire; mortars and machine guns were sweeping all the ground in front of me. We had been warned that nearby explosions could perforate our eardrums, so I lay as flat as I could with my mouth open and I held my hands over my neck under my steel helmet. But as soon as I could I began to crawl back towards our front line although it seemed every weapon the Germans had was being used against me.

Several times as I crawled, I was lifted off the ground by explosions and I couldn't hear after the first few. I became very confused as I wasn't sure which way to go. My nose and ears were bleeding and I was finding it hard to breathe. I have no idea how long it took me to get back to our forward lines and when I did, I couldn't hear anything that was being said to me. Stretcher bearers took me to the Regimental Aid Post where the Medical Officer gave me some treatment. It was there that I was first de-briefed by our IO. When the intense barrage began the CO informed Brigade HQ immediately that he had 'stood to' the battalion, expecting a major counter attack. Experience had shown that such attacks were usually preceded by a heavy 'stonk'.

The IO had known I was in their line of fire and thought I was already dead so he was very surprised that I had managed to get away. As I was still bleeding, I was sent back to the Field Dressing Station to be assessed for further treatment but was able to return to the battalion next day. Then I made out my logbook report and was de-briefed again for any further information.

In subsequent days, several POWs were questioned to find out if they knew if any high-ranking officers had been killed whilst visiting their area but I was never told of the results. We snipers were never informed of how significant our actions were. Later the CO told me that they all had the definite opinion that I had shot and killed a very senior officer for such a massive barrage to be unleashed on me. Whilst it was possible I had perhaps killed a very popular officer it was more likely that he was extremely high-ranking and was advising his Orders Group on tactics. I wondered if my shot had changed their battle plans and caused some considerable chaos. Questions about the integrity of my report were upheld by the Brigade Intelligence Staff later on, who said that the duration and massive retaliation barrage they laid down on me was unprecedented.

Although Harry was a teetotaller, his CO handed him a mug half full of rum on his return which he was grateful for, and told him he was not to go out again until he had recovered. In fact, the experience left him suffering from mild shell-shock caused by the heavy concussion of falling shells. His hands were shaking uncontrollably, his vision was blurred and he was stone deaf: none of them physical pre-requisites for a sniper. After two days he began to feel better and was able to hear speech, although he thought it was a week or so before his hands were steady again. He did not believe at the time it had any long-term effects, but did admit that subsequently he flinched far more under shellfire than he used to do, which was hardly surprising. It was from this period that he began to experience the effects of being under continual stress, having flashbacks and going over and over past events in his mind.

> Sometimes very late at nights if I couldn't sleep, I thought about that particular incident, as over the campaign I had sniped very many enemy soldiers, most of whom were priority targets such as officers and NCOs. I was always extremely careful to avoid attracting any attention to my concealed position, and so I didn't shoot very often at ordinary soldiers unless I considered them a real danger to me or my mates. I preferred to wait for my targets, for when privates moved about, it often meant that higher ranks would expose themselves. Which was their mistake. I never ever found out the rank or identity of the officer I shot, nor did I ever really want to know. It doesn't do any good to learn such personal details for any operational sniper. It was a rotten job but a necessary one in war.

The Hallamshires entered the rolling farmland east of Caen and the advance proceeded without pause for ten days. It was very different to the earlier fighting, with nothing but continuous movement for the already exhausted troops and it introduced a new form of open warfare to the snipers.

> We marched along with all our gear, weapons and ammo, iron rations and everything we needed to sustain us in action. Heavier weapons such as the Brens and light mortars were passed down the columns so each of us had a turn at carrying them. On long hard marches, it was quite possible to have a short snooze as you marched, with your mates keeping you gently in line as you closed your eyes for a few minutes' shut-eye. We all took turns at this method of resting. It was a strange fact, but the steady action of marching and changes of direction around bends etc.,

could all be coped with in this manner. At stops, we were all basically keen to keep moving as resting for too long stiffens up your legs and it is much harder to get going. At a rest we would lie on our backs if possible and put our legs up against walls or trees or suchlike to let the blood circulate better ... anybody tending to wobble from exhaustion on long marches would get immediate help from his mates, NCOs and officers, who would take over their equipment and weapons for a while ... you quite often saw officers carrying two rifles and double the amount of personal load, so that way all coped.

After so much relentless combat, the effects of what has now become known as 'combat stress' were beginning to be more generally observed. There were very many names given to the condition by the soldiers, though 'bomb happy' was probably the most common. Whilst Harry was never taken out of the line because of it, he admitted that it became a constant and unwelcome companion for the rest of his combat time.

> There were many riflemen who simply became useless, and a few snipers suffered from it too. Often, they had the shakes, or they jumped like cats at loud noises, both of which, of course, were hopeless for accurate shooting. Some simply broke down and were whisked away by the MO because it was very bad for morale, but at least it was understood and treated, unlike in the Great War, when so many exhausted men were shot for cowardice. After my brush with the German artillery, having shot their senior officer, I was never quite the same. I lost some of my composure and did find that sudden noises rattled me. Some men simply became more fatalistic, saying 'If it's got my name on it ...' but if anything, I became more cautious. I think being so highly trained helped us snipers and although we were under great stress, we were free agents to a large extent so avoided the daily grind of the infantry.

The causes of shell-shock are many and complex, but the mental make-up of the individual is a significant determining factor and it was clear that Harry was fortunate to have the mental strength and conviction of his training to avoid the worst effects of the problem. Whilst not engaged in the type of intense fighting they had previously experienced, the snipers' lives were, as usual, anything but peaceful: they were constantly investigating, checking and observing, then returning with reports and assessments. More frequently, they were being asked to take other specialists with them, which placed an even greater burden on their shoulders.

> When an artillery forward observation officer requested to be taken forward to a specific position, then it was usual for the sniping NCO to carry out the task, as it was most likely he would have already been well forward of the lines, and knew the best routes in and out again, usually coming back via a different route in case they might have been spotted going forward. These forward-moving patrols often took up a considerable time, for it was nearly always quite impossible to take the shortest route to a specific position. It often entailed crawling slowly using a long detour so as not to attract any attention to the site you wanted to end up in for observation purposes. At all times camouflage was essential and use of cover as much as possible. Moving forward this way presented many problems [if we were] not to attract the attention of enemy observers who were continually watchful for our snipers moving into position.
>
> We tried, if possible, to avoid water, for lying up all day long in drenched clothing is an added hazard. As well as adding discomfort to your worries, in cold weather as water dries it steams, and that alone can give you away to a skilled man with binoculars. We didn't ever wash beforehand, as the smell of soap is very distinctive and, of course, no sniper ever smoked. Sometimes we had to wade, particularly when we got to Holland, but did so only if there was no other course of action.
>
> Then the farmers out in the open country frequently had layers of barbed wire around fields to keep their cattle in, and often these wires were tangled inside the hedges, etc., making it difficult to crawl through; both farm and wild

animals can and do give away your presence. So great care had to be taken anywhere near animals.

Only when you have to crawl a considerable distance does it become apparent just how many problems you face trying to avoid detection. Once spotted it inevitably brings down immediate counter-fire. And if the NCO was going forward with a FOO who made any mistakes, then the consequences could be very bad indeed. It was our responsibility to ensure that in taking out these artillery observers we brought them back again in one piece!

Occasionally, there were times when the role was reversed and the infantry were able to save the snipers, albeit unwittingly. One night, while snatching a brief sleep in a small foxhole, Harry was suddenly woken by heavy gunfire right next to his position.

I remember being in a trench when a German patrol, in pitch darkness, was driven off by our Brens. It was only at first light that I noticed an unexploded German grenade on the very edge of my trench.

Crossing the Seine, 20 August

The Hallamshires continued to push the Germans back, with this stage of their advance consisting mainly of short, sharp firefights, with Allied armour constantly pushing the Germans east to the Seine. Crossing this wide river posed a major difficulty for the fleeing Germans, as due to Allied bombing there were now no bridges, leaving them with virtually no means of continuing their retreat. Undeterred, they formed very effective rear-guards using MG 42 teams and snipers working together along intersecting firing lines, with anti-tank guns sited in strategic places, and minefields in between. The Allies were far ahead of their own heavy artillery, so they used what tanks they had, as well as the infantry A/T guns. This was the situation when the Hallamshires were brought up to dislodge the defenders from the Forêt de Brotonne west of Rouen, which was proving impenetrable to the tanks.[9]

Our infantry were moving up the bank of the river, but we snipers were told to assist in clearing the wood, as it was proving very hard for the snipers of the other battalion (KOYLI) to deal with them. We moved up to the edge of the wood, and were given a briefing by their sniper sergeant, who said they had lost several men, as the German snipers in the wood were extremely good. What was planned was to absolutely soak the wood with mortar fire which it was hoped might drive the Germans back. We were to go in as sniper pairs with a Bren gunner allocated to us. We had not worked like this before, but apparently it was a tactic that worked very well in jungle fighting when the snipers would search for targets and the Bren gunner would rake the area either killing the sniper or flushing him out. I have to say, it was not a brilliant plan, but I suppose there was little else that could be done at short notice.

The wood was chaotic, with fallen trees and branches everywhere. German dead were in foxholes and once or twice we were held up because we couldn't tell if they were actually dead or not. There was some sniping and we retaliated, and it was the only time in the war that I shot a German in a tree, although if he was a sniper or simply an infantryman I never knew. We were always instructed never to use trees, but apparently German training doctrine was to use them when possible. What prompted him to do this, I have never understood, but my number two spotted a movement in the branches. Myself and the Bren gunner fired simultaneously, and he tumbled down like a sack of potatoes. Mostly the Germans seemed to have withdrawn after the barrage but the battalion captured a lot of them, as they were surrounded as they left the wood.

Harry also witnessed an uncommon piece of battlefield chivalry:

It can be said that the snipers from both sides built up a deep-seated respect for each other's abilities and never, ever underestimated their opponents in a duel. With sniper against sniper there is never a second-place winner in … duels. Both sides habitually shot any snipers they captured. It was reported that US General Omar Bradley was heard to say that he would not take action against anyone 'that decided to treat a sniper a little more roughly than they are being treated at present'. However, on one occasion a lone German sniper had got very close to our Battalion HQ when he was spotted, shot at, wounded and unable to escape. Very quickly a German stretcher party appeared with an NCO carrying a red cross flag to collect him.

One of our sentries at the forward OP didn't know what was expected of him, so let them continue and take away the badly wounded sniper. As soon as Batt. HQ found out they were furious, as they badly needed a prisoner to question, but they accepted the sentry had acted as an act of chivalry, so nothing further was said about the incident.

The pressure of the advance had to be maintained, regardless of the effect it was having on the combat soldiers who were soon to experience another unpleasant crossing.

I recall clearly a feature that we had been warned would cause us great trouble, a dominating hill that we locals all called 'Snigg Hill' after a well-known landmark in Sheffield, but in the event we crossed and rode up with the BGCs to find no opposition, not even a lone sniper. We were quite pleased about this, as you can imagine, and it appeared that the Germans had slipped away during the night. We put out a couple of observation patrols, and two of us went forward before dawn to look for signs of activity and I think we got as far as Vieux-Port where there was a very active rearguard waiting for us.

I had the fright of my life here. I had crept upstairs to find a good spot from which to snipe, and as I opened the door on a landing, immediately a German soldier behind the door jumped right over me, knocking me to the landing. At the same time the German fell down the stairs in obvious fright but then managed to run away. I thought it likely he would bring more soldiers, so I too had to scramble out fast to find an alternative place to conceal myself.

The advance now stopped on the banks of the River Seine, at this point a deep and very wide body of water that was not going to prove easy for either army to cross. In something akin to the Dunkirk spirit, the retreating Germans commandeered sixty-odd boats of all types and made a successful night crossing of the river, thus saving most of their retreating army. But, like the British at Dunkirk, they were forced to leave behind almost everything in terms of equipment that could not be physically carried.

> We had an interesting time at the river, as there were tons, literally tons, of equipment and vehicles, artillery etc. lying about. During the fighting many in the battalion were keen to secure a good war trophy. It was strictly forbidden to loot, of course, but the thin line between war booty and what we termed 'liberating' was a margin often overlooked, and so it was not only the rank and file that were on the scrounge for war souvenirs, but a few officers were keen not to be left behind. Certain items of enemy property were high on everyone's list of personal 'wants' and that involved any cameras the Germans carried. For although they could use them freely on the front, and did so, we British were under a strict rule that we couldn't use cameras or have personal diaries in case we were captured and the information might be useful to the enemy. Nevertheless, we still looked for cameras which we might be able to send home. Especially high on our wants list was any type of Leica camera. Then we wanted pistols, binoculars and suchlike.
>
> It was all forbidden fruit, but as soldiers playing a deadly game in which life itself was cheap, most were prepared to bypass a few regulations at that period in our life. It became common to see the lads of the rifle companies of all ranks carrying pistols tucked into their web belts. And we all knew that any choice goodies could be quickly sold for British pound notes or American dollars to the American soldiers. I never recall any of our soldiers finding a Leica, but one of our captains did 'liberate' a fine Zeiss Contax camera. The reason that I remember it well is that the captain used up the film still in the camera by taking photographs of his men and he also got a few of us from the sniper section ... it was the only photo ever taken of the Hallamshire snipers

in the line. No doubt he sent the camera home. But we never saw any of the photos he had taken … I would very much like to have had a copy of that particular photo of me where I could be seen with all my mates.

After crossing the Seine and advancing steadily eastwards, the battalion reached the town of Crèvecoeur-le-Grand. Intelligence reports stated that it was strongly defended and this proved to be the case. 'C' Company of the Hallamshires suffered very heavy casualties in attempting to cross the bridge into the town. The next morning Harry was called to see his IO and asked to undertake a patrol towards the River Vie to determine exactly what the situation was. He left before first light, safe in the knowledge that at least no lurking Germans would still be on the Allied side of the river. Nevertheless, he was his usual cautious self.

> I camouflaged up and left before dawn, only carrying the minimum of kit, as this was an intelligence exercise, and of course I carried my rifle, but only necessary ammunition. I had my Scout Telescope and note book and had been told speed was of the essence. This is a juggling act as being in a rush leads to mistakes, but on the other hand it was imperative that the information I obtained was passed back as fast as possible. The previous assault had given no reports of enemy on the west bank of the river, so I took something of a chance and made my way overground, keeping to cover as much as possible, but I must say not as slowly as I would have liked. There was sporadic mortar fire landing nearby, and I guessed that from somewhere I was under observation, but they must have been quite a distance away.
>
> When I got to a clump of trees close to the river, I could clearly see that the bridge had been blown up, but I could not see any signs of the Germans. A couple of abandoned vehicles, but no movement at all, which was puzzling. I watched solidly for half an hour, but not a single person was sighted and eventually I reached the conclusion that they had gone, so returned as fast as I could and reported the fact to our IO. He asked if I was absolutely sure and

> I confirmed the facts, so he went to confer with the CO and I was stood down.

The results of this patrol proved to be considerable. The battalion pioneers were ordered forwards and were able to find a narrowing of the river nearby at which they built a temporary bridge out of telegraph poles and planks. This allowed the infantry and all of their vehicles to cross the river. Harry's part in this is not mentioned at all in the war diary, although several awards were subsequently issued for the crossing. As he remarked resignedly, 'We snipers were always out of sight, out of mind when it came to awards.'

Le Havre, 10 September

The next major operation for the Hallamshires was the attack and capture of the port of Le Havre, codenamed Operation Astonia. Le Havre, like Caen, was vital as a safe port for landing supplies and reinforcements. It was expected that resistance would result in heavy Allied casualties since the port was extremely strongly defended, so in an attempt to prevent a bloodbath, the commanding officer of the German defenders, Colonel Eberhard Wildermuth, was offered conditions of surrender by the British, which he rejected. Hitler had sent him a 'fight to the last' order and on the face of it he appeared to be prepared to obey it. None of this was known to Harry of course, whose officer had warned the snipers that they must be prepared to deal with a lot of MGs situated in the pill-boxes. Harry and his squad had devised a specific means of doing this.

> Our instructors who had fought in the Great War had told us that we had to work closely with the infantry to defeat pill-boxes. The best means was for us to put very accurate fire into the apertures to prevent the German machine gunners from shooting. This enabled the infantry to work round them to the rear or right underneath the apertures from where they could throw in grenades then rush the entrances. The problem was that these emplacements often overlooked each other, with a firing aperture covering the centre ground and back entrances of the two in front. It required careful co-ordination and we needed to find

good positions from which to shoot. We did not know how hard this might be as we had little information about the defences other than there were a lot of them.

We went on a couple of patrols with, I think Lieut. Pearce around the big Schneider Works. This was hard work. We were being shot at from concealed positions along the road including by multiple 20 mm cannon. I tried to find a place from which I could shoot at the Germans, but the ground was mostly open and eventually I hid behind some huge steel rolls in the yard. I managed to pick off a couple of machine gunners but the crew of the cannon were too well protected and it was getting very hot there. Several Hallamshires had been killed there and I decided it was no place to stay, but then, I suppose you could say the cavalry arrived! Several of our Churchill tanks appeared and began dealing with the enemy positions in a very methodical manner. I suppose it took an hour, but eventually resistance ceased and white flags began appearing. As we began to mop up, we heard huge explosions from close in front of us.

There were demolition charges placed on all of the bridges across the river although a Hallamshire major and his corporal had managed to disconnect one, leaving an intact bridge for the attacking troops.[10] Harry and two other snipers were asked by Colonel Hart Dyke to accompany a party over the bridge to clear the dock area, and he saw an unusual incident there.

> We crossed the bridge and were grouped along a ditch. I was looking through my binoculars for targets when the CO was talking to another officer, Lt McNeile, when he dropped like a stone.[11] He was shot right between the eyes, a true sniper's shot and everyone dived for cover. I tried to spot where the sniper might be, but some of the riflemen had already spotted the position and under Bren gun cover they ran forwards. Amazingly they came back with two live camouflaged German snipers, for I fully expected them to have been shot. I heard they were taken away for questioning, but I don't know if they ever made it back as far as HQ. The men were pretty angry about their officer.

It was a sad end to a successful day, for the Hallamshires had played their part in taking Le Havre without the expected losses. One reason was that in holding out for what appeared to be a reasonable length of time and then agreeing a surrender, Colonel Wildermuth felt he had more or less adhered to Hitler's orders without sacrificing his entire garrison.

There was an amusing finale to the capture of Le Havre, for aside from over a thousand German prisoners, the battalion uniquely also claimed as booty one submarine and three Dornier seaplanes. Harry's day also ended on an unusual note, for when he returned to HQ he was amazed to find everyone looking unusually merry.

> At first, I thought the war might have ended, but it turned out that the men had 'liberated' a huge stock of champagne from somewhere and everyone had been guzzling it, and even the officers were quite tipsy. As I didn't drink, I wasn't really party to it, but it was funny seeing everyone reeling. I heard the CO wasn't best pleased as there was no hot food because the cooks were all too drunk!

Apparently, this incident was eventually taken in good part by the CO and no disciplinary action followed. It was a harmless, albeit rather undisciplined method of releasing stress and remained a much-talked-about incident at regimental reunions long after the war. For the snipers and other infantry, this was a well-earned chance to stand down and they rested for nearly a week in La Cerlangue, just east of Harfleur, where the townspeople held a service of thanks for the Hallamshires. It was a brief interlude of relaxation that Harry always remembered with gratitude, because it also gave him a chance to repair some equipment deficiencies and mix with the townspeople.

> We had been under constant stress and hard fighting for weeks and it was good to feel that the French appreciated what we were doing to liberate them. None of our boys needed to buy a drink and local people often invited us in to eat with them, which as they had so little was very generous of them. We supplemented their food with our rations. We knew that there would be a lot more for us to

contend with in the coming months but for a while there were no patrols, or sleepless days. In fact, the first night it was so quiet that I couldn't sleep, though I think the next night I slept for fourteen hours solid.

Aside from rest for their weary bodies, there were all the usual unavoidable tasks to attend to.

> The constant wear on our clothing and equipment was just something we had to live with, as there was no means of replacing anything in the line. It had taken a week for me to get a new pair of boots but they were considered essential items of course. Other things were not so vital, like my Denison smock which had holes in the elbows from constant crawling and resting on them when observing. Our unofficial regimental tailor found another torn smock and made me padded elbows and he put leather inside then sewed camouflage cloth over it, which was very practical as it helped cushion the elbows. My trousers, too, were in a state, the knees were torn out but I was able to get a new pair, although I have no recollection of how. The CO was very protective of his snipers and I think he had a hand in ensuring the QM was able to find whatever was needed. My binoculars and telescope both had dirty lenses, where moisture had collected inside, but they could be dismantled with care and cleaned.
>
> I do recall one of our snipers had a damaged scope and had asked me if he could use my No.2 rifle, and although I was very reluctant to hand it over, he was simply not operational as a sniper without it, and we were short-handed. I don't recall exactly how long he had it for but when he returned it, I must say it was as clean as a new pin. His replacement [rifle] had arrived. It was the only time I ever lent a rifle to someone else.

There were the usual debriefs for the snipers, new intelligence reports to read and recce photos to study. The rest was certainly justified, for the next objective was the tough approach to the Belgian border and then the advance into the Netherlands.

Chapter 5

Belgium and the Netherlands

AFTER THE VARIED TERRAIN OF FRANCE of *bocage* and then huge open-field systems, the British troops advancing east into Belgium and the Netherlands were facing yet another form of warfare, which at times was to prove almost aquatic. Belgium was quite densely populated and there were even more villages to be fought through, but for once the men of the 49th Division found little actual fighting work to do by the time they arrived, and so they happily rode in convoy through Belgium towards the Dutch border. Moving an entire battalion, and all its weapons, stores and so on, was a tremendous logistical feat, requiring over 100 vehicles and the snipers travelled with the HQ transport across parts of the old Flanders battlefields to a town named Nijlen, just inland from Antwerp, although this wasn't carried out without some unexpected casualties.

> There was a hazard that none of us expected as we drove through many of these towns, and that was being hit by the items thrown to us by the local townspeople. Mostly it was flowers but often there were apples and pears which were like rocks. All of our snipers and HQ staff thought it very funny when I got hit in the face by an apple that gave me a lovely black eye! We soon learned to keep our helmets on, and tipped over our eyes because it was possible to have been quite badly injured, but we couldn't blame the people for their enthusiasm.

Whilst in the area, on 23 September, the battalion saw waves of towing aircraft and gliders passing overhead, although they had no idea where they were bound for. This was the airborne armada heading for Arnhem with its ill-fated consequences.

Eventually the trucks stopped at a village called Lille, same name as the French city but this place very close to the Dutch border. There they de-bussed and were instructed to prepare for an advance the next day, 24 September. The first major obstacle facing the advancing XXX Corps was the Antwerp–Turnhout canal and an attack was planned combining Canadian and Polish divisions. As with the assault on Le Havre, this was expected to be met with stiff resistance and the snipers were well prepared, having been briefed that their primary task would be to clear the surrounding woods and farms. This indeed proved to be the case, as enemy small-arms fire was very heavy and the German artillery barrage was one of the heaviest anyone in the regiment had ever experienced.

> It didn't take long for the Germans to react. To live through these savage bombardments and the very intensive firing, is something most of us snipers will never ever forget, for once they ranged on the likely areas we were operating from, then the entire locale was plastered and we could only hope we might live through it. I found that in hugging the earth that everything I wore got in my way – we even had the idea that buttons were too thick! If I had on my two web ammo pouches then I always made sure I had them widely separated so that I could get close to the earth as I was pounded with debris. It became a habit that I would consciously keep my mouth open during these massive counter-fire barrages, as I was aware that it helped slightly to preserve my eardrums which otherwise could have been blown. As it is I still suffer from a perforated left eardrum.

Harry's sniper section was then involved in attacking the north-west corner of an objective called the Depôt de Mendicité at Merksplas, a huge, solidly constructed series of nineteenth-century brick buildings that was a combination of poorhouse and charity institution. It had latterly been used to house Jewish slave workers but it was also a perfect defensive position for the German forces. But unlike the capture of Le Havre, which had eventually proved comparatively easy, it became clear from the very outset that this was certainly not going to be the same. The attack stalled very early

An early twentieth-century postcard, pre-1914, of the Dépôt de Mendicité. The complex was huge and the Hallamshires and other attacking units took two days to clear it completely. Every window was a potential vantage point for a rifleman, sniper or machine gun.

on, at the perimeter of the Mendicité, until Corporal J. W. Harper of the Yorks and Lancs rushed forwards, leading his platoon in a very cool assault which cost him his life, but won him the VC.[1] This attack distracted many of the defenders so 'A' Company with Harry's snipers crept up on the buildings from the opposite side.

> We could see that there were riflemen inside the building, as well as machine guns. So, I started a methodical sweep of those visible. We were behind a wall, at a little under 200 yards, so it was perfect for shooting, though the Germans put several bullets so close to my head that I heard them crack as they passed. I kept shooting at any target that presented itself, and our Brens raked the windows. In fighting such as this the concept of 'tallies' became meaningless. Although each shot was carefully placed there was no way of determining if I killed or wounded anyone, it was impossible to tell. It was a little like shooting at a booth, as a target appeared then disappeared, but eventually our

> weight of fire enabled us [our infantry] to cross the open ground and get into the buildings. We snipers were not equipped for close fighting like that, and remained where we were, shooting at any German who appeared. We could hear the sub-machine guns and grenades bursting. At one stage a pair of Germans with an MG 42 ran towards some outbuilding. I think three of us fired simultaneously and they dropped like stones.

By nightfall, the complex had still not been completely cleared, but the sniper section was pulled back to get some rest and replenish their nearly exhausted ammunition. It took another day of fighting by the infantry and the help of some Polish Sherman tanks finally to clear the buildings. This marked an end to the fighting that the Hallamshires were to do in Belgium, so from the end of September to 3 October they bivouacked in the woods just west of the Depot. Harry spent some time looking round at what the Germans had abandoned and found a snipers' hide that had evidently been well-used:

> It was very cleverly dug into the rising ground between some large trees, which must have been hard work, as there were big roots there and it was very well covered with logs and branches. There was a firing slit built in at an angle to our advance and the view was excellent. Inside there were many spent cartridge cases, ration tins, and a very detailed hand-drawn map of our lines, showing the distances in metres from the firing point. I took this and kept it for many years afterwards. There was also a very nice camouflaged jacket hanging on a nail, with a hood and it appeared to be reversible. I was very tempted but wearing captured uniform was dangerous, as you could be mistaken for a German and shot, or if you were unfortunate enough to be captured, they would assume you had taken it from one of their dead, with the same end result. In fact, it was also the reason we never, ever used captured German weapons, particularly sniping rifles. For snipers there was no way of knowing how a rifle had been sighted up or what state the barrel was in and as the war progressed, we even heard

> tales of rifles that were booby trapped. The infantry did use German Schmeissers, often preferring their high rate of fire to their Stens. Of course, the danger with this was that in a confused combat situation, the sound of one of those firing was very distinctive and could result in retaliatory fire from your own infantry.

A few days later the battalion moved eastwards, Harry remembering with pleasure that they were able to ride on the back of the Sherman tanks and bask in the engine heat that blasted out of the ventilation gratings. The Hallamshires continued to follow the Polish Armoured Division for another two days, heading towards the Dutch frontier and helping them to clear out pockets of resistance. Harry said that this period was something of a blur, as they advanced very fast and all they knew was that the Dutch border was very close. They were surprised when they crossed it, for it turned out the Hallamshires were the first unit of the division to do so, a fact of which Harry was totally oblivious until he saw some of their own Churchill tanks dug into defensive positions on the Dutch side of the border, and he thought 'My word, we *have* come a long way since June.'

His main concern was to link up with his HQ Company and as usual, catch up on sleep. Tactically, the situation was changing, as more German reinforcements began to arrive and organised resistance stiffened. This took the form of counter-attacks across the front, many of which had to be beaten off. The fighting began again in earnest at Aarle-Rixtel, north-west of Eindhoven, where an infantry section covering a bridge was attacked by three German tanks. Harry and another sniper were in position, and although incapable of knocking out a locked-down tank, they could sometimes have a surprisingly effective method of dealing with them.

> During German tank attacks, our snipers were all kept very active, for in their initial movements it was not unusual for the tank commanders to look out of their open turret hatches so that they could observe the advance clearly, for when they batten-down all their hatches they travel in a

semi-blind manner. Hallamshire snipers were successful on several occasions in eliminating tank *commanders* from battle. On this occasion the commanders were not visible, so we fired at the vision slits, which contained prisms. If struck, they shattered, leaving the driver without any means of seeing where he was going. I do not know if we helped, but one of our A/T guns managed to knock out the lead tank.

The type of fighting was significantly different because the snipers were now instructed to work with the Allied tanks in the face of a potent German anti-tank weapon that from mid-1943 was increasingly being seen in the front lines. This was the Panzerfaust (literal translation 'Armour Fist'),[2] one of the first of the subsequent large family of infantry-operated anti-tank weapons. If aimed at the wheels of a tank it would shatter the idler gear, rendering the vehicle helpless for follow-up hits. If the engine compartment in a

A well-concealed German with a Panzerfaust 60. These had a range of 200 ft (60 m) and the 15 lb warhead could penetrate 8 in. (200 mm) of armour, more than any Allied tank carried. Despite this, only 6 per cent of lost British tanks were destroyed by them, but their ease of use and portability meant that their threat required constant infantry and sniper support.

Sherman was hit, the results were usually unpleasant, for the fuel tanks would inevitably ignite, incinerating the crews. This gave rise to their grim German nickname of 'Tommy cookers' or 'Zippos'.[3] It seems strange that snipers should be working so closely with tanks, but there was a good reason for this, as Harry explained.

> Our own ... support tank squadrons were now very vulnerable, not only to enemy snipers when advancing with their hatches open, so whenever it was possible our sniper section moved forward to take on specific targets. These included the brave German 'tank killers' as they called themselves. These Panzergrenadiers would wait in concealed positions until our tanks were actually passing them, then they would attack with their highly portable Panzerfaust. They had a heavier version that could deal with any of our tanks at that time, plus they would sometimes actually get onto our tanks as they went forward and fasten mines with short fuses, and even attempt to fire their Schmeisser submachine guns into any open vent. One of our sergeants used his Sten gun literally to hose two Germans off the back of a tank, which they were trying to ignite with petrol. At times we used to take prisoners and some of these tank killers had emblems stitched onto their uniform sleeves to show how many tanks they had personally destroyed.

As the Allies advanced, resistance gradually stiffened and they became aware of a very different attitude on the part of the opposing troops, as there were many more Waffen-SS units facing them. They were uncompromising fighters, usually very experienced – and they rarely surrendered. Yet there was a paradox, as it was also apparent that there was a noticeable increase in the number of ordinary German infantrymen who appeared very willing to surrender. Harry commented that it was at times like fighting two different armies and he was of the opinion that, for the ordinary soldiers:

> ... all the fight had been knocked out of them, they had suffered so much on the Eastern Front and could see the direction the war was going. Our advance appeared unstoppable and many must have wondered what they

were continuing to fight for. They were not fanatics like the Waffen-SS men.

What struck Harry most forcibly about their new location was the increasing presence of what the Netherlands was famous for, water. As the snipers helped to dig out positions for their HQ, they struck the water table only a few inches below ground level, rendering the construction of any form of slit trenches an impossibility.

> I hadn't realised just how wet Holland was going to be, not only underfoot, but also in terms of weather; we seemed to spend as much time fighting that as we did the Germans, and there were times when the rain won, hands-down. It was miserable, because not only was it nearly impossible to dry out – our clothing was not waterproof remember, but we couldn't take shelter from the shells or mortar fire, so great care was taken in trying to find places that were on slightly higher ground and drier, where we could dig trenches. Mostly we tried to use the many scattered farms that were everywhere, but had to be careful because of booby traps. It also played havoc with our rifles, as they had to be kept oiled to prevent rust and often there was no rifle oil to be had. We used to beg engine oil from the reconnaissance company, filling up our little oil bottles which we carried in the butt-traps of our rifles. To try and keep the rifles protected, we always oiled the bores, but before every patrol we ran cleaning patches through them to clean out any slightest residue of oil as we did not want barrels 'pluming' to give our positions away.

A considerable amount of fighting was to be done through the many small villages and isolated farms that were dotted about this area on small parcels of high ground, and Harry had an unwanted adventure at one that tested his nerves to the limit. The Hallamshires were advancing methodically across open flooded country, heading for a small town, the name of which Harry could not recollect. As they moved cautiously through the seemingly empty streets it was, as normal, the task of the snipers to keep to the flanks and eliminate any enemy resistance in the form of machine gunners, snipers, or anti-tank squads. Harry spotted a German soldier with a Panzerfaust hiding behind a wall and he slowly moved into a position from where he could take a shot. Having dealt with the German, he realised that, in the time this had taken, he had lost contact with his infantry party. Let him continue the tale.

> I lost the direction of the section I had been following at a crossroads and as I ran to try and catch up, I spotted what I thought was a burned-out German tank; it had that look about it of having been on fire. In a street maze you have to be fast to avoid enemy fire so I ran zig-zag to the tank and got underneath as temporary protection before running on. Suddenly I was aware I could hear German being spoken from inside the tank … so it wasn't a knocked-out tank at all! Thinking it would bring machine-gun fire onto me as I left the cover, I just had to run as fast as I could again to get round a corner. I stopped … to risk a quick look to see if they had a hatch open in case I could get a shot at anyone looking out but it was all closed down so they mustn't have known I had been underneath. With only my 4T rifle there was nothing much I could do as the tank started up again and moved off.

It was an incident indicative of Harry's professionalism that instead of running as fast as his legs could carry him to a place of safety, he paused to see if he could inflict any damage on the enemy vehicle. He said later that he regretted not carrying armour piercing ammunition that day, as he would have fired at the tracks to try and break a linkage!

The Hallamshires advanced deeper into south-west Holland, heading towards the major port of Rotterdam. This fighting along the Scheldt estuaries was particularly hard for Harry's snipers for they were dwindling in numbers, as death and wounds took their inevitable toll. He said of this period that at one stage they were down to four working snipers and took willing volunteers out with them to help with observation work. There were also some novel reinforcements in the shape of the 104th US Infantry Division, which worked with the 49th Division. Harry said of the Americans that they were good combat soldiers, although he never met any of their snipers, but all of the British infantry were in awe of the equipment and rations that the Americans had, particularly the rations! The Americans were always keen to buy souvenirs and a lucrative trade sprang up between the British and US soldiers and Harry's sniper section soon became the proud owners of several boxes of K-rations, specifically designed to provide high-energy food for the troops. Harry said that whilst they had no practical use for captured helmets, pistols or spare binoculars, they did have a real need for as much food as they could get hold of; happily swapping souvenirs for K-rations proved to be ideal. Besides, these ration packs had the added benefit of having very practical combustible packaging.

> We were shown that if you set light to the carton, which had a form of protective wax inside it, it would burn long enough to warm a tin of stew or heat a cup of soup. Also, it created hardly any smoke, and although we never used it in a hide, it was very good for a quick hot meal when we were back from patrol. The British would have done well to have copied it, but they never did.

The Scheldt, 2 October

The ever-present water became an even greater problem in the Scheldt region, as much of the low-lying farmland was now badly flooded due to German demolition of protective dykes and sluices. This gave rise to one of the few stories extant about another sniper team of Harry's section, which subsequently passed into regimental folklore. Harry takes up this remarkable tale:

> We were in an area where the German Army had blown dams and dykes to slow our advance, it was only the buildings on slightly higher ground that were above water … the Netherlands are fairly flat, so the water was rarely more than six feet deep in parts, with lots of areas waist-deep and less. Snipers going forward on their patrols could sometimes wade to positions they had selected previously

from our survey maps and aerial photos from Intelligence, and for the deeper areas we went out with supporting fighting patrols in rubber boats so that we could get a dry landing. It was normal to go out just before first light and, if we went by boat, to be collected again after dusk so we wouldn't be spotted by enemy patrols or snipers. To be left on these 'islands' gave a high risk factor, but it was the only way possible to operate at the time.

Sniper Metcalfe[4] who incidentally had given very creditable service as a sniper since the beach landings, was alone and well forward in one of the few dry areas, when suddenly a German fighting patrol also landed from a boat and began to sweep the area to try and find snipers. Metcalf knew it would be a sudden end for him if discovered and began a deadly cat and mouse game as the Germans probed everywhere. With no further places left to hide, he made a break for it to attempt to swim away from the patrol who by then had spotted him and were rushing to cut him off, leaving him with no time at all to plan a secure escape. He rushed … across a mudbank in which he lost his waders, he threw his sniping rifle into deeper water to prevent them taking it to use against us later, and began a swim for his life as the patrol started to shoot. It was an incredible escape against all odds, and it was only one of the incidents from his service that caught the attention of the Dutch government when it was reported back.

In fact, there was more to this tale than Harry was aware of, as two snipers were involved in this incident, having been hiding in a ruined farm from where they had observed German soldiers gathering at a small village nearby. They took a calculated risk and fired a red flare to call for artillery support. This brought forth a heavy and destructive mortar barrage on the surprised Germans, who immediately realised that they must be under observation and their patrols would soon have surrounded the pair and killed both on the spot. With nowhere left to go, they both dived into the water from the dyke, despite wearing full combat clothing and wellington boots. The flood was particularly deep here and they amazingly survived a fusillade of enemy gunfire by keeping underwater for as long as they could. They reached the British-held dyke and were brought back, shivering with cold and barefoot. Naturally, the first attention they were given was not medical but hot sweet tea well laced with rum!

The slow advance continued, with villages gradually being cleared house by house, and Harry lost count of the times he went forward on a lone patrol to try and seek out a German sniper known to be hiding somewhere close by. He recalled that it was highly demanding and utterly exhausting work. Sometimes, the infantry would find themselves under fire from the rear, as a lone German sniper who had remained undiscovered tried to increase his tally, but attempting to find him was usually futile, as the Germans were experienced enough to fire only one or two shots, then make a fast escape. By the end of October, the Hallamshires had reached the curve of the Antwerp–Turnhout canal for the second time, almost a month to the day from their first crossing.

There was one incident that Harry recalled from this period, when the Germans brought up a Panther tank to try and force a passage through the village of Wuustwezel. There were no 6-pounder A/T guns available and an officer[5] decided to take on the beast with small arms. On a tank as large and heavily armoured as this, it would normally be as effective as firing a pea-shooter at it, but fortunately the Hallamshire snipers were at hand and were asked to try their trick of blinding it by hitting the observation prisms or visor slits. To everyone's delight and amazement, Harry included, they managed to do this with such success that the tank withdrew.

> We were very rightly pleased with our work and when we returned to HQ, the CO came and personally thanked us for what we had done, which, I can tell you, meant a lot to all of us.

As they waited overnight in the small town, Harry collected his second wound which was, coincidentally an almost direct duplicate of his first.

> A sudden barrage dropped on us from 'Moaning Minnies' and I received a right leg wound ... a large chunk was sticking out of my leg above my right knee. I managed to hobble back to our RAP, and again was sent to the nearest Field Dressing Station where they soon removed the main chunk of embedded metal, but it had fractured into tinier pieces inside my leg. Again, after only a few days treatment and rest I reported back to Battalion HQ, albeit limping a little.

It was not until he arrived back with the unit that he realised that something was amiss with his rifle.

> I always laid it down flat, because a rifle leaning against something could often fall hitting the scope and that might affect the zero. When I collected my rifle, I saw the scope was not sitting square on its mountings. I looked closely at it and decided that I must have landed on it, or it had been knocked when I suffered the blast from the shells, although I was not aware of it at the time. Luckily, my No. 2 was at HQ so I collected it and found our REME sergeant who reckoned the mounting bracket was bent. I had to leave it with him to sort the problem out, which did not take long.

By the end of October, the battalion had moved into a very wet area, with the city of Roosendaal posing a major stumbling block. The Germans had been reinforced by several tough Waffen-SS and armoured units, and resistance had once more stiffened considerably. The town was cleverly defended with dug-in tanks and self-propelled guns, all well camouflaged and with overlapping fields of fire. The enemy machine-gun teams were sited in between these zones, and any infantry advance was well-nigh impossible without having very well co-ordinated supporting armour and heavy artillery back-up. Harry's memories of this fighting were very mixed chronologically, as one firefight merged seamlessly into another, but he recalled an advance into the outskirts of the city, where they waited while watching rocket-firing Typhoons strafe the German positions.

The Typhoons were both terrifying and amazing, and we agreed that none of us would want to be under a strafing attack from one. Their rockets were huge and could shatter any German tank, and I believe they carried four cannon as well.[6] We watched them pound an SP gun position which had been causing quite a problem as it formed a road-block on the main road into Roosendaal. We moved up behind our tanks and there was virtually no opposition, but I leave it to your imagination what the German positions looked like when we got there. Most of the defenders had been blown to pieces and the vehicles were almost unrecognisable.

We snipers thought we'd got off very lightly but then we were ordered to go to HQ which was in a cellar of a house and deal with snipers in a windmill several hundred yards ahead. It was dark by then so we left before first light and set up an OP in a small copse. The Germans in the windmill seemed to consist of one or possibly two snipers and a machine-gun crew and they had a tremendous view. We guessed they were probably protected by road mines to stop our tanks but there was no way we could check this without being under direct observation.

I was with Sniper Les Pickering and we decided the best tactic was to deal with the snipers first, then the MG crew. We kept well back in the cover of some trees and watched. The Germans clearly did not think there were any British soldiers nearby and one of them was smoking. Pickering took him on, and I shot another who was visible at the large doorway half way-up. The MG opened up at once, but was firing blind, as he didn't know where the shots had come from. It was situated behind a sandbag wall quite high up, so we both fired quite low, as a .303 bullet will easily penetrate a couple of thicknesses of sandbags.

It suddenly went quiet and we sat and waited, but there was no movement, so we scurried back to the recce platoon and they sent a BGC up. We stayed with the infantry but when they got into the windmill, they reported two dead Germans and a machine gun with a badly damaged mechanism. So, our shooting had been very accurate!

> Incidentally, I should mention of Pickering that ... he had a remarkable ability to remain awake around the clock at times, and he was highly reliable when forward in vulnerable areas of our front. He was one of so many. And now, so long after the war, it is hard to recall all the names of those first-class snipers, NCOs and privates who were such valuable members of the sniping section.

Harry was greatly surprised by his reception when they returned to HQ, for the RSM looked at him wide-eyed and blurted out 'But you're dead!' Apparently, much to everyone's sorrow, the death of a Corporal Furness had been reported, but it turned out to have been a closely named Corporal Furniss.[7] Harry's chums in the sniper section were more prosaic about his return, commenting dryly that his timing was bad as they were just about to help themselves to his K ration packs!

As the Hallamshires advanced, it was necessary to dig into a new position once or sometimes twice every day, an irksome but vital task. This left no time to obtain creature comforts, but the further they advanced into Holland, the more obvious it became that the resident German soldiers did not suffer from this problem, and seemed to assume that their stay was going to be a long one. The British have always had an idiosyncratic sense of humour, more so in wartime when, the tougher things became, the more frequently black humour was used to lighten the mood.

> Can you therefore imagine our surprise as we advanced and captured ever more enemy positions, to find out just how well planned and semi-luxurious they frequently made their firing trenches etc.? It was a real eye-opener for us and we shouted with laughter at our finds. The German soldiers just didn't hesitate to grab whatever suited them from the houses and properties in their sectors and so they lined their nice deep dugout–trenches with carpets, blankets, cushions and whatever took their fancy to make themselves comfortable. It was an idea too good to overlook, so at times you could come across 'well-furnished' Hallamshire slit trenches. We never considered it to be looting, merely borrowing for a while, for we always left the comforts in the

slit trench when we moved on. It didn't end with small rugs, blankets etc., for some soldiers with a developed decorative taste added various other items and I remember one Hallamshire squaddie sitting in a slit trench wearing a top hat he had picked up somewhere.

Was I any better you might ask? I'm afraid not. We dug in near some shell-battered houses, smoke still rising, where we gathered together a few 'comfort' items to line our slits. There on the ground by a house I found a clock, probably thrown there by the blast, and it seemed right to add it to my own trench furnishings. I soon found out it was a musical chiming clock that on every hour played a lively tune. At the time I didn't know what the melody was called, of course, but it fascinated me and I kept it on the top edge of my slit trench and I kept turning the dial fingers to hear the tune again.

It wasn't long before the squaddies in the nearby slits complained, but I took no notice and kept repeating the tune I was beginning to like. I'd just put it up again on the top, when somebody shot it and it fell on top of me, but I put it back again, still playing. That resulted in shots from several more riflemen who all wanted to join in the fun. It fell in the trench, all broken up and we were all laughing our heads off by then.

For some time afterwards, the Hallams would ask 'Where's your clock?' So, someone's pride and joy got shot up by the Hallams as a way of relieving the tension we were all feeling. Long afterwards, I was able to identify that particular tune as being 'Fra Diablo'[8] ... a tune I won't ever forget.

The Hallamshires continued heading eastwards along the course of the Rhine which was by now within sight. The river was their eventual objective, but they had to take the sizeable village of Oudemolen first. The problem for them was that the level of casualties they had already suffered meant that they were now seriously short of men, to the extent that their anti-aircraft unit had been disbanded and the gunners co-opted into the infantry. The regimental war diary commented that the fighting here was 'the most difficult encountered in the whole campaign across North-West Europe'. There was no way around these objectives and the flooded land precluded anything but a full-scale amphibious landing, which was impossible due to lack of vehicles, so they had to be captured piecemeal by frontal assault. The snipers were paired off to work with the advancing infantry, operating on the flanks to deal with the greatest threats, but things did not go smoothly for Harry and his partner. Unusually Harry wrote this account in the third person, but this was because his innate modesty prevented him for mentioning that both he and his colleague received a Mention in Despatches for this outstanding piece of work.

> The two snipers worked as a pair ... moving from one position to another after firing; it was usual to move often in case an observer had spotted a muzzle blast, etc., and brought down fire on our position. Suddenly the area became alive with German infantry moving forward, so [the snipers] quickly moved into a shell-damaged house to hide. They went upstairs and got into the rafters, just as a section of German infantrymen also moved into the same house. After only a hurried glance in all rooms, the Germans settled down in the lower ground floor, making it impossible for them to escape. There was no other option but to settle on the exposed rafters and wait, but in the meantime, they used binoculars and the Scout Telescope to observe the area. It was a couple of days before the infantry moved on, meanwhile the two men took it in turns to snatch a short rest in between keeping out of sight, but they did manage to compile a very useful log of the identity of German units, plus their equipment etc., which they were able to bring back to Battalion HQ. In the meantime, it had been thought that they were missing in action.

It took the battalion until 5 November to deal with the last defenders here, many of whom were Dutch Waffen-SS who had no qualms about fighting to the death and often proved to be fanatical. Harry noted how rarely they were willing to surrender, and witnessed one incident in particular that remained firmly in his memory:

> As we advanced through Holland we had been moving very quickly, a large farm was in front of us with the company intending to bypass it ... but a platoon was left to clear the farm. I got there with my team mate as our platoon were taking up positions to move in. But I was just in time to catch sight of a German soldier on the ground pulling himself and a Spandau machine gun backwards into a small lean-to by a barn. I called to the platoon NCO and pointed to the lean-to, and we all fired into the place at the same time. It was fairly riddled with our bullets. It seemed he meant to delay our advance and certainly, if I hadn't spotted him first, it is very likely he would have badly shot-up the platoon as they moved against the farm buildings. I was told later that the much shot-up soldier was a senior NCO of the Dutch Waffen-SS but from his choice of hiding place it must have been obvious to him that he would never leave the place alive.

Their progress through enemy-occupied Holland was not without its pleasures, for the populace were thrilled beyond words finally to be liberated by Allied troops. One such town was approached very cautiously, but nothing human or mechanical appeared to be moving. Unbeknown to the Hallamshires it had already been abandoned by the Germans. Harry's men, slowly working around the edge of the suburbs, were alarmed by a sudden commotion, loud shouting and cries, but from where they were they could not see the cause of it. Tense and ready for trouble, Harry and the riflemen carefully pushed their way through a garden and between two houses to be met with a sight they were not expecting:

> In the middle of the road was a crowd of women, maybe thirty or forty, and they were making a tremendous racket, shouting and crying and completely surrounding our advance party. The officer was trying to get the Bren gunners to cover the road, but no one could move for hugs and kisses! Eventually it was understood the Germans had long gone and the women insisted on giving all our men drinks. I thought it was very funny and wished every town was as easy to liberate.

The division had a well-deserved rest at Roosendaal, which, because of the exhausted state of both the Allied and German troops, was spared the intense fighting that would normally have occurred and this halt allowed the Germans to slip away. However, heavy British losses were still a serious concern and to ensure the men remained in fighting condition, every combat soldier was given two days behind the lines, one for a 24-hour sleep and the other to shower and obtain clean clothing. This included the snipers of course and Harry remembered with pleasure 'not feeling utterly exhausted and being clean again. We also got as much food as we wanted and caught up with letters and parcels from home.'

Off to the south-east the Germans had formed a very strong defensive line on the west side of the River Maas near Venlo, forming a long narrow salient. It was therefore vital to capture this ground if the advance was to continue towards the land between it and the River Rhine. To achieve this, the 49th Division and its Hallamshires were transferred to Second British Army.

The division was once again very lucky not to be involved in the heavy fighting to capture this salient, but on 24 November it took part in the attack on Venlo, a large city on the edge of the River Maas, close enough to the German border for it to be under fire from the Siegfried Line.[9] Intelligence reports from patrols including Harry's snipers, confirmed that, as usual, hundreds of 'S' mines had been laid in the open country and small woods on the line of advance and the routes were well covered by MG units. These mines were obviously highly dangerous to advancing troops, and they also provided an early warning of an attack to the defenders, as well as being extremely time-consuming to locate and remove. Harry spent a considerable amount of his patrol time finding and digging up these little killers, laying them to one side to try and form safe paths – but as he said, it wasn't his job to deal with the mines, simply to make the routes the snipers used as safe as possible.

> We arrived in the woods but there was not the amount of fire coming from them that was expected. We were all very wary by now about abandoned positions, for the Germans now routinely booby-trapped everywhere and they were

very clever. We had been issued with a cruciform spike bayonet for one reason only, to prod for mines and look for booby traps. I used in preference my Fairbairn-Sykes knife's thinner blade which slid in easily at an angle, whilst I very carefully prodded for mines. There is absolutely no doubt that my FS blade saved my life several times over as I found I was crawling into a mined area, a very typical hazard for a sniper. My blade was therefore a life-saver. So even when I was wounded and was in two different field dressing stations, I made sure I hung onto my FS blade, and that's why I still have it.

The intelligence details that Harry and the other snipers took back to HQ were of great help in determining where these minefields were. To help lessen the huge problem an innovation was introduced during 1944 in the form of armoured troop-carrying vehicles called Kangaroos.[10] Their primary quality was the ability to traverse minefields sown with 'S' mines without casualties as, when triggered, the mines flew into the air to about human waist-height before detonating and were not hazardous to passengers in the Kangaroos. The much larger anti-tank mines were not normally dangerous to infantrymen, requiring a heavy pressure to detonate them, but they would slow down an advance for hours and pioneers did sterling work in detecting and removing them before an attack. In this they were greatly helped by the use of flail tanks[11] which proved hugely successful in clearing these minefields.

The Hallamshires were pleased to be given seven Kangaroos to ferry men across nearly a thousand yards of open ground towards the woods on the outskirts of Venlo. Harry thought they were a wonderful thing and a long-overdue invention, as they allowed the infantry to close fast with the enemy without heavy casualties and their speed made it very difficult for German artillery to register on them. Their big drawback was that, like any tracked vehicle, they could not enter woods so that pleasure was entirely left to the infantry.

The German troops were by now very well versed in British tactics and knew that the first thing the advancing Allies would do was push their snipers and observers forwards, so they left behind well-prepared hides or foxholes that were death-traps, all being rigged with very cunning booby-traps. Harry had one golden rule for these positions.

> If it looked too good to be true, then it was, and I avoided them like the plague. Most of the riflemen following up were wise to this by now, although some got caught out. Sometimes explosives would be linked to a timer, and the whole thing would go up hours later.

He found he had little work to do but make patrols, as the advance through the area was unexpectedly fast due to the lack of serious opposition. The Hallamshires pushed on, meeting little resistance until they entered the Nijmegen Salient, where they rejoined their division, once more meeting up with the First Canadian Army.

Nijmegen and the Islands, December 1944–March 1945

There could be no let-up in the Allies' relentless advance but this period was particularly bad for infantry casualties because the Germans had laid 'S' mines in their thousands and the snipers found it very difficult to work in their normal manner. Harry mentioned that they could only go out with pioneers who had mine detectors and the clearing of the mines was a maddeningly slow process. Many of these very brave pioneers became casualties, losses that the battalion could ill-afford. The unit was now very close to Arnhem, where the last stages of Operation Market Garden had taken place, and they finally arrived at the bridge over the Nijmegen canal. This was so close to the German lines that they could hear the Germans talking. Harry was billeted as normal with HQ Company, in a region that became known as 'The Islands' due to the flooded ground. The geographical location of Nijmegen and its bridge were of great significance for both sides, for it was on a small island formed where the Rhine split in two, creating the Rivers Waal and Nederrjn that flow to the North Sea. Because of the flooding, the towns on either side had been built on the only high ground in the region which meant that holding them provided the defenders with a panoramic view across the landscape. So it became imperative that the Allies took control of the bridge and its towns as quickly as possible.

> We arrived there at the beginning of December and it was a miserable time for everyone, especially we snipers due to the snow and wet conditions. It was a peculiar place because we were under the view of the Germans every time we needed to get to or from the HQ building as we had to climb a bank. I have no idea why [HQ] decided it was a good spot but we snipers were forbidden from operating from there as the retaliation would have caused havoc. However, we were told to set up a watch system on the river as it was believed that German frogmen would try to destroy [the bridge] but that was countermanded and a Bren team took up station instead. We were quite happy about that as it was extremely cold and snowing!

There was some compensation, though, as it proved a fruitful time for sniping and they had unexpectedly cosy billets. When not in the lines, the snipers took shelter in the cellars of local houses that were on the edge of the fighting zones, although in the snowy and wet January weather even these cellars often flooded slightly, as the water table was so high. Harry recalled that it was like living in a World War One dugout, as they had to have duckboards on the floors to keep themselves out of the water, but it was far easier for them to get out on patrol and the cellars provided both secure and relatively comfortable quarters. Early morning patrols were hard work, though, as stiff bodies had to be coaxed into action, and daily Harry crawled laboriously to his hide to observe and make notes. Patrols were mostly out of the question, for the snow and water made even the stealthiest of movement nearly impossible, and the snipers knew they were under continual German scrutiny.

Shooting at targets from carefully constructed hides would normally have proven counter-productive, but often Harry was occupying positions that had quite exceptional visibility over the enemy positions.

> Some of the damaged houses had an open view across the flat landscape and in the very cold light I could see

for miles with my 22× scope. Even the T/S appeared to be more powerful in that light, and I took a few careful shots at long range – over 500 yards – scoring several hits. The Germans could never work out where I was, as I was set well back in the roof-space so there was no smoke from the discharge and I had a lovely strong beam to rest the rifle on. I had asked Parker-Hale to make me a special 'Y' fork spike … I used to use it at times in sniping from darkened building interiors when I used to ram it into a table top or chest of drawers away from a window. I could rest my rifle on it near to the magazine (never the fore-end or the barrel).[12] I was waiting for long periods for a target to present itself.

Sometimes it was so still and quiet that it was hard to imagine there was a war going on. We were constantly on patrol, either with infantry, or in hides covering them from snipers or possible MG fire. It was exhausting but also rather odd, as we would return to our warm cellars and be given hot food and be able to sleep rather well. One of our snipers said it was like going to the office every day, but instead of pushing paper we were potting Jerries.

The snipers were rested for the week before Christmas but were back in the line on Christmas morning, as there had been no let-up in enemy activity with constant mortar and artillery shelling. The battalion was then ordered to establish observation outposts on the north side of the Wetering canal, which was easier said than done, as every approach was very well covered by three enemy MG posts. Harry takes up the story:

Colonel Hart Dyke asked us to see him and we were shown a map of the area, with a brickworks shown, and he asked if we could reach it and 'set up shop' to deal with the MGs and German snipers. We said we could, so we hatched a plan for four of us to go out before light and take a small path up to the brickworks. This was made easy by the fact that there was a lot of snow about so visibility pre-dawn was quite good and in preparation we put on the white snow suits we had been issued. We got into the brickworks by taking out a lot of bricks from the rear – and it was slow work moving them, then hiding them behind us so as to make sure we did not leave any signs we were there. Eventually we made hides for ourselves, working in two pairs about a hundred yards from each other. We had to be as quiet as possible as sound carries a long way in still snowy weather.

We watched the houses opposite and were rewarded by seeing the shutters open slowly as it got light. We were all ready to shoot and did so more or less simultaneously. I know we got two of them, another disappeared into the house, but, oddly, there wasn't a peep from the machine guns. We had to assume that they had withdrawn as they felt too vulnerable with us there, and the brickworks became a regular snipers' position for the whole time we were there.

The CO was so pleased with the result of the snipers' work that he again personally thanked the whole section. The only downside was that the Germans began to shell the brickworks in a very methodical fashion in an attempt to dislodge the snipers, but the Hallamshires' pioneer section had worked hard during the nights to create more space inside them, within which the snipers were virtually impregnable, utterly impervious to mortars and safe from all but the very heaviest of artillery. Neither Harry nor his fellow snipers had any inkling whatsoever that their shots from here were to be the last they would fire in anger.

On 25 January, the Hallamshires were ordered back to Nijmegen for a rest and the issue of leave passes which were handed out, enabling those who wanted to go to Brussels. Harry declined, preferring to rest and attend to his chores, but he did recall watching the launching of V-1 and V-2 rockets from some distance away. He remembered wondering where they would land and if any would be able to reach Manchester.

The rest soon came to an end and the battalion moved eastwards towards Zetten in the first week of February, which was characterised by more heavy snowfall. This proved a serious hindrance for the snipers, as it was too deep to move through, so their usual patrols around the flooded landscape had to be undertaken in canvas boats. Two snipers had a lucky escape when theirs was holed by an obstacle and they fortunately made it to a small area of high ground, but were then marooned. In the sub-zero temperatures, swimming would have brought death by hypothermia and they dared not fire Very lights, as it would attract unwanted enemy interest. One man solved the problem by using his shaving mirror to signal 'SOS' to the British lines and a sharp-eyed artillery observer spotted it, directing a DUKW[13] vehicle to them. Their return to the sniper's bivouac was apparently greeted with loud quacks.

Despite these difficulties Harry and his comrades were able to continue their clandestine work. Sitting in a ruined house to observe enemy positions one morning, they were amazed to see a German patrol working their way along the street outside, looking for any signs of British activity as they methodically went from house to house:

> ... throwing in a grenade, then following up with their Schmeissers, although as far as we knew, the only people here were us and our signaller. We stayed put and eventually they came into our house, but didn't stay long and very strangely didn't open fire, then left. It was a great temptation to shoot them, but that would have given the game away as it was a very useful OP but when we returned that night, we reported to the IO in case they were waiting to ambush British patrols.

The weather had begun to thaw, which was not at all helpful to the soldiers as it brought more flooding to the already saturated ground and created thick mud, but fortunately for Harry and his section, their work in this sector of Holland was just about finished.

In early February, patrols were sent out to determine if the enemy were holding the opposite bank of the River Wetering in any strength, although, as always, nothing could be done in the way of an advance unless it was with the use of amphibious vehicles. Harry and fellow snipers were holding some unenviable posts in front of the British line, in conditions that Harry recalled vividly as being:

> ... quite the worst we had been in. It was bitterly cold and because the snow had melted, our hides were constantly

Hallamshires on board a DUKW arrive in 'The Islands' near Zetten, Holland. The level of the ground water can be gleaned from the fact that normally the road was well above the water table.

> waterlogged and once in position, we had no choice but to remain there until darkness. We could not warm ourselves, eat or drink anything hot or even move position very much although at times I had cramp and had to straighten my legs. It had to be done very slowly, which as anyone knows is exceedingly painful if you have cramp. Any need to deal with nature had to be done in the hide so we tried not to drink too much during the day.

This static warfare was not set to continue because, on the night of 21 February, a big joint British and Canadian amphibious assault was finally launched with the aim of capturing the towns in between the Rijn and Wetering. This was a very hazardous operation indeed, as it was known that the Germans had the area under close observation. The sniper section had been boosted by the addition of another six men, raising their complement to eighteen. Several were newly trained and required careful watching, but there was an immediate setback when two were lost almost immediately after a counter-attack by the Germans, who managed to wipe out an entire platoon of 'B' Company holding the village of De Hoven near Dordrecht. Harry was not detailed for that specific operation which was extremely fortunate, for the war in Europe was about to come to an abrupt end.

Arnhem – The Last Battle, 12 April 1945

The battalion was rested after the fighting on the river, but as ever 'rest' was a misnomer, as Harry commented.

> There was no doubt we were all completely shattered by then. We were functioning like automatons; we ate, slept when we could and looked after our kit, but it was in a sort of haze and everything was an effort of willpower. A short rest was not sufficient to allow anyone to recover but we knew we were finally on the last lap, although when and if the Germans would surrender was a matter of much discussion. I do not recall anyone saying that they were fed-up though, I think we all just wanted to get the job finished and the Germans beaten and there was a great will amongst the army to make that happen.

Gradually, the flood-waters were beginning to recede and another advance was proposed to drive the enemy completely out of the Wetering area using the flail tanks. The Hallamshires were now at the very edge of the Rhine and sniper patrols were cautiously pushed out to glean what information they could. The next plan was to launch a crossing using both DUKW and Buffalo[14] amphibious vehicles under a heavy artillery covering barrage on the rear areas at Arnhem to prevent any reinforcements coming up. Harry, the HQ staff and snipers crossed in a Buffalo and the one incident he recalled was once again seeing RAF Typhoons as he put it 'absolutely annihilating' some enemy positions. The vehicles landed on the German side of the river and moved forward immediately to clear the town. The snipers were called up to deal with a persistent

German MG post that was firing from a concrete tower but by the time they arrived, firing had ceased and there was no sign of the enemy. Their observations seemed to confirm intelligence reports that the town was no longer defended by any German soldiers. Then there was a sudden halt to the fighting in the face of a quite unexpected humanitarian request from the Germans.

> Arnhem in Holland was twice a major battleground … in September 1944 which didn't end up in our favour due to overwhelming numbers of elite German infantry backed up by an equally large number of support artillery and tank squadrons. But there was also a second major battle to seize Arnhem in April 1945, in which my battalion played a major role in the assault.
>
> Again, we faced elite German forces in great numbers so the battle was extremely fierce but we were successful in capturing the town along with a large number of prisoners taken. As a sniper I was extremely active as I flanked our attacking rifle companies, but I wasn't to know then that I was actually taking my part in the last major assault of our campaign across North-West Europe. In our sector there was a noticeable slow-down in full-scale battalion attacks as the Germans fell back towards prepared defensive positions … it was mostly a case of sending out fighting patrols, whilst I operated on our 'Sniper Shield' covering our own forward positions against enemy patrols and German counter-patrols.
>
> We advanced and took over front-line positions in an area we knew as 'The Grebbe Line'[15] and facing us some few hundred yards away were our old enemies, the volunteer Dutch Waffen-SS. At this stage of the war which we were winning, it seemed to us that these Dutch volunteers knew already that life for them would not be pleasant if they survived, so instead they were more than willing to fight to the death. They proved, in fact, to be elite fighting troops, ruthless in action, but so were we on our side.
>
> From memory it must have been the beginning of May 1945 we held the Grebbe Line, when a party of German

officers made contact under a truce flag to talk with our senior brigade officers. They informed our officers that the Dutch civilians in that entire region were on the verge of starving.[16] As the conflict had prevented any supplies getting through to them by road, the German troops, who intended fighting on, didn't want the civilians to suffer unnecessarily. They agreed that they would allow large food supply convoys through their lines without any interference, and offer any help needed. In return we were informed that if we advanced any further during this truce, they would open all the remaining dykes and flood the entire region, just as they had done previously in parts of Holland. Our rear headquarters quickly arranged the food convoys, and they went through without any problems.

The Hallamshires' battalion commander knew of a proposed ceasefire but was unsure if any of the German soldiers were also aware of it, or exactly when or if it might occur. So exploratory patrols were still being sent out to reconnoitre.

We [snipers] were still highly operational with patrols going out, at that time I took up my usual flank position ... and before first light I had entered a farm building to find a position in the rafters where I could observe a wide area of our front. I found a long ladder which I used to climb up to just under the roof slates and opened it up sufficiently so that back in the shadows I could view the front. I remained there over a long period, just using mainly my Scout Regiment telescope in its usual ragged wrapping to camouflage its shape. For some hours I saw no movements from the enemy troops, but I continued to scan the area using either the telescope or my binoculars for a wider view.

I suddenly saw movement behind a long row of bushes which bordered the roadway. As I watched intently, I soon saw that it was three German soldiers although at first, I didn't get a good view of what they were doing, then I made out that in fact they were laying mines, most probably anti-tank mines to catch our tanks if they broke through those bushes. The squad of three, an NCO with two privates must have been from an engineer unit, but I was in no hurry to start shooting, for I was experienced enough to realise that usually mine-laying squads have somewhere near them for protection a two-man squad of machine-gunners, so I started searching all round … to see if I could spot their position. Which I knew would be more than likely to be camouflaged.

It is not wise tactically to shoot from a concealed snipers' position if you know you might be under observation yourself, so I knew that in attempting to shoot more than once, to drop the NCO first, then take fast follow-up shots at the two privates, would immediately mean a protection squad would quickly observe my muzzle-flash and then blast the position with automatic fire. Typically, I stuck to the idea of firing only one shot, at most two, from any one position after which I always moved to a pre-determined alternative concealed position. But on this occasion, I was considering firing up to three fast successive shots which is very risky, but as I couldn't spot a possible back-up squad it was a calculated risk that I considered worthwhile.

I had just put down my binoculars and picked up my 4T rifle to look through the telescopic sight, when I heard a noise behind me. But as so many of our soldiers were around, I wasn't duly concerned as I looked back towards the high ladder I had used. I saw the grinning face of one of the officers from the nearby rifle company. I think it is important to reiterate here that when a front-line area is fairly quiet (it doesn't happen often) it was always wise to let the senior officers of any nearby rifle company know beforehand that I would be taking up a concealed position in their area. The reason being that if I spotted a worthwhile enemy target and fired, then it wouldn't lead to an immediate stand-to in their forward firing lines; they would be aware that it might just be a sniper shooting.

I told the officer I was about to take-on a mine laying squad and that he should come over to look at them. He lay down next to me and looked through the tiles I'd moved, but as I raised my rifle to sight and shoot, he leaned forward and pushed my rifle barrel down.

Some of the first Dutch civilians liberated by the Hallamshires in Ellecom, 14 April 1944. Harry recalled that the Germans had fled and the inhabitants were trying to come to terms with being liberated.

Now, after so many years I no longer recall his exact words, but it was something like 'No, leave them alone, it's all over.' I just stared at him in surprise, for previously nobody had ever told me not to shoot; it is always entirely the decision of the sniper whether to shoot or not. That young officer then told me they had just received from our CO a message via the company RT set that we were to stand down, that a ceasefire was due at any time.

What he told me was breathtaking news, I just couldn't believe it. I was told to get my gear together and come down to join all the other soldiers who had started gathering. Suddenly, I was overwhelmed at the thought that the fighting was over. I realised that against all odds I

> had survived as a sniper during a grim campaign. It was as if a huge weight had been lifted off me. The other soldiers were all the same, they couldn't find the right words to say, so some started shooting in the air as a means of relieving their tensions. Then we heard incoming enemy mortar-fire, whether or not the German artillerymen were aware of the cease-fire I do not know. But for those three most fortunate German soldiers ... all went home safely, I hope, to live happy contented lives with their families. Yet on other parts of the frontline an assault was officially supposed to start at 8 a.m. the following day.

Harry's colonel was indeed correct, for the German commanding officer had agreed that all fighting would cease promptly at 08.00 hours on 5 May 1945, with all German forces in Holland surrendering. Nevertheless, the Hallamshires continued to move cautiously forwards, passing through Arnhem to a town called Ede and on 7 May they arrived in Utrecht, where they were told that the war in Europe was indeed officially over. If the soldiers were bemused, the inhabitants of Utrecht certainly were not and they erupted into the streets with flowers, bottles of wine and beer that had been carefully hidden throughout the occupation, in what the battalion history termed 'a carnival atmosphere'. Mindful of his earlier black eye, Harry kept well back in a truck, watching with amusement as women threw flowers into it, and occasionally persuaded the not-too-reluctant soldiers to give them a kiss.

> We were welcomed by cheering masses in their thousands, it was joyous chaos and confusion, for there amongst the crowds were still large numbers of heavily armed German troops, who seemingly were without any orders so didn't know where they were supposed to go. It was only later that we started to disarm them and got them moving in long lines towards Germany. Just before we entered the city ... I thought it best to dismount my telescopic sight and place it for safety in the fitted metal case which I slung over my shoulder, and I carried my 4T rifle on its leather sling at my side ... so I was careful to preserve it from damage, for by then the massed population were singing and dancing

as we attempted to march in order towards the city centre where we were received by the city VIPs and our own waiting generals. From amongst the crowd, a pretty girl approached me and with a smile she placed a single flower into my rifle barrel, for which I thanked her; somehow it seemed significant.

It was only later in retrospect that I thought about those oh-so-lucky German soldiers I had under observation in my telescopic sight and was about to start shooting. It was fateful that one of our officers with such perfect timing had come to my hide with the news that we were all to stand down and cease operations, for I knew that it would have troubled me later if I had targeted them just as the war ended. Yet on other parts of the frontlines where the news of the ceasefire had been delayed through difficulties, we became aware that still soldiers on both sides lost their lives, such is war.

Of this period, Harry had only one further comment to make, and that was in respect of his much-revered commanding officer.

The pity of it was that the CO, Colonel Hart Dyke, was not with us, as he had been replaced a month or so before. He was a perfectionist, a genuine hard-task-master who did everything 100 per cent plus himself and he expected at the very least that each soldier in his battalion must do the same. There was no leeway, no half-measures for him, but his methods paid off in action and so he was held in great respect by all. I am of the opinion that if he had asked us to follow him into Hell, we would all have done so with no hesitation.

Chapter 6

Aftermath and Later Life

The Occupation Army, 1945–47

THE CESSATION OF FIGHTING left a strange atmosphere hanging over all of the units who had fought so hard, for so long. One described it as a 'sort of breathless feeling, like you were waiting for something to happen, a bit like a thunderstorm' and few could completely believe that the war really had ended. The Hallamshires were ordered to continue into Germany as part of the Army of Occupation but now they travelled all the way in the comparative luxury of their lorries, watching the peaceful countryside roll past them. Harry spoke of the peculiar feeling of seeing a landscape untouched by war, with neat houses and well-tended fields. There were no burned-out vehicles, no ruins and the all-pervasive smell of the dead had vanished. It seemed hard to believe that the war had touched these rural farming communities at all, and even the larger towns appeared undamaged by bombing.

> We all kept to our routines of making sure our rifles were clean but we were at last able to oil up our rifles and barrels to help protect them without worrying about using them the following day. By this time, I had been promoted to sergeant so was in charge of the section, although aside from making sure we looked smarter than we had done in combat, there was little to do as we simply drove through Germany.

But, as they approached Duisburg, they began to appreciate the colossal scale of the Allied bombing campaign, as there was hardly a complete building standing, and most were simply piles of burned-out rubble with hurriedly cleared roadways between them.

There was a damaged barracks near the city allocated to house the men and they occupied a part of it with other units from the 49th Division. Some sort of organisation was urgently needed to aid the civilians, and much effort was spent in trying to alleviate the plight of the thousands of refugee Germans, many of whom had fled the advancing Red Army. They slept in cellars or crude shelters made of corrugated iron and desperately foraged for food during the days but there was little to be had. It was not Allied policy to inflict suffering on German civilians now the war was over and great efforts were made to bring in food and medical supplies, the Berlin Airlift being the culmination in 1948 after Soviet forces blocked all access to the city. In the early months of the occupation, however, no such organisation existed and the situation was utterly chaotic. Many soldiers, Harry included, gave the civilians their spare rations and the Regimental Aid Posts, now no longer needing to deal with the wounded, opened up to provide medical help for any who needed it. It clearly upset Harry, who spoke only a little about it.

> We couldn't help but feel so sorry for those starving civilians and all our men tried to help in some way, in particular they couldn't bear to see the children suffering. Many were in rags of clothing and very undernourished, Hitler wasn't their fault and it seemed to us that they did not require any more punishment.

Within a few weeks, the sniper section was disbanded, as there was no longer any requirement for it, all except Harry being transferred to other duties within the battalion.

> I was selected by the CO to take up the appointment as Battalion Musket Sergeant and to work closely with Captain Simmil who became the Battalion Weapons Training Officer. Together we worked very closely with Regimental Intelligence. However, because of these movements I lost contact with my former companions in the sniper section, much to my regret, especially now in old age. I had by then been awarded an oakleaf insignia [signifying a Mention in Despatches] for my sniping services.

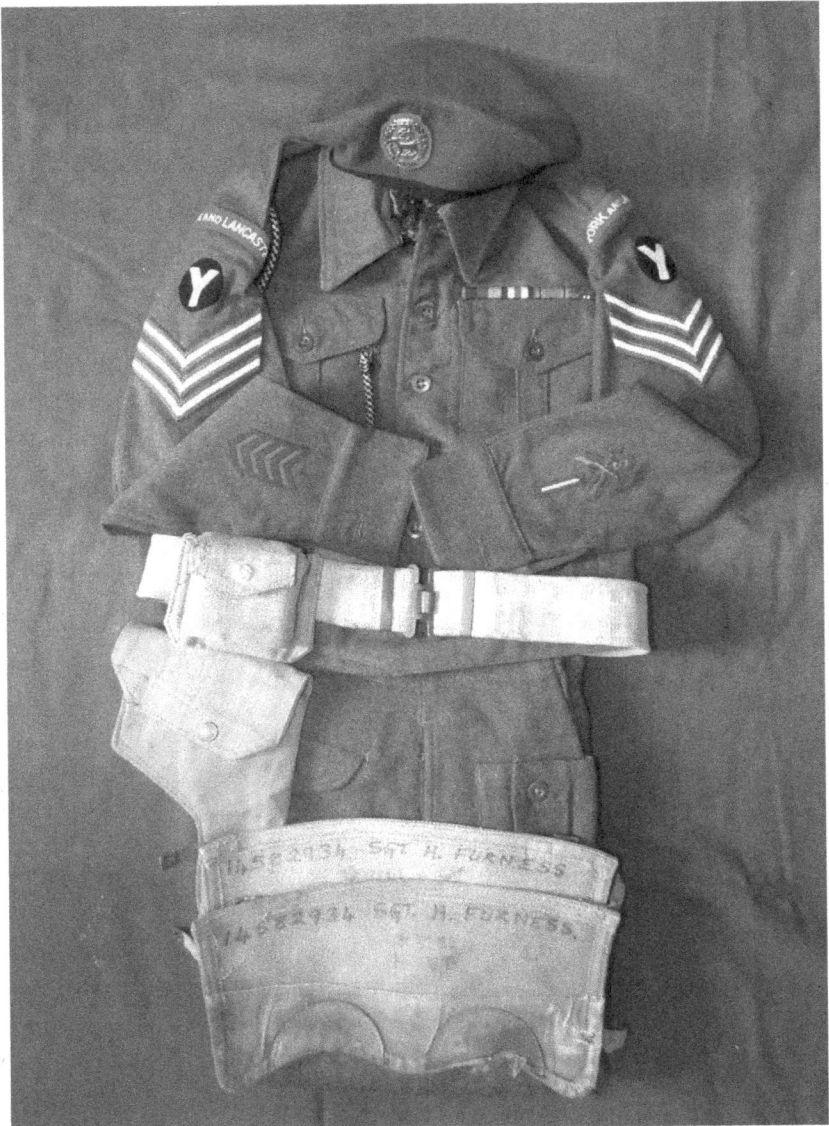

Harry's immediate post-war uniform showing his four-year service stripes, wound stripe and sniper's badge. His medal ribbons are the 1939–1945 Star, France and Germany Star, Defence Medal and 1939–1945 War Medal with Mentioned in Despatches oak-leaf clasp. Post-war the 'Y' divisional patch replaced the Polar Bear although the cap badge was unchanged. The belt, holster and gaiters were wartime equipment, the brasses on the belt being green-painted. The backcloth is actually a military blanket that Harry brought home. It has the texture of steel wool.

The battalion began to settle down to peacetime duties, and gradually its manpower was reduced as men were demobbed, eventually being brought down to a little over 100 officers and other ranks. Patrolling was unnecessary so Harry created a rifle training course to keep the men interested and occupied, but he also had some more unusual duties. Partly in an attempt to help out the hungry local population but also to provide something different for the soldiers to eat, the Control Commission, the overseeing Allied governing body in occupied Germany, suggested that it would be a good idea to permit the hunting of deer in the large forests that abounded in Westphalia. They realised that not only did the herds require culling, as managing them had been neglected during the war, but there was the added stumbling block that those civilian German gamekeepers who had returned from the army (mostly former snipers) were all prohibited from owning rifles for the unfounded fear of reprisal attacks by hardline ex-Nazis. Initially only Allied officers were given permission to hunt but only a very few had the experience to do so. The majority were not schooled in stalking, and none had the knowledge to shoot telescopic-sighted rifles.

> … it turned out to be a complete and utter disaster, simply because the officers were not trained in riflecraft, and very few had ever been near a wild game hunt. Officers had turned up demanding I hand over sniping rifles for them to use (at the time I kept all the telescopic-sighted rifles). I was very reluctant to loan out specialised rifles but was out-ranked, so I gave them a brief lesson and told them NOT to attempt altering the elevation/deflection turrets, but of course they returned the rifles, and no deer, with scopes badly re-adjusted and incorrect for short distances. They managed to wound a few poor animals, which got away, or missed entirely. The German foresters (all of whom had been disarmed) bitterly complained and insisted that the cull must stop … so it happened that the high-ups at the Control Commission ordered that only trained snipers should hunt, and I was selected.

Harry was thus given special permission by his new CO, Lt.-Colonel C. K. Halford, to cull as many deer as he could, the idea being that half would go to the locals and half to the resident troops. While this worked very well for the Germans, who were used to eating venison, the idea was quickly abandoned for the British.

> No count was made on how many deer I killed, but it was a lot and certainly about [equivalent] to two large herds. A professional German forester acted as my guide and a platoon of Hallamshires followed in Bren Gun Carriers and loaded the dead deer, which they took directly to the nearest German town hall, who distributed the venison among local butchers. We only ever kept a couple of deer back, one for the Officers' Mess and one for the Sergeants' Mess ... I do recall the cooks ruined the venison as we ate them right away, when they should have seasoned them by hanging for a few days. But I still like venison!

This unwittingly brought him into conflict with a new regimental sergeant-major, who saw Harry returning from a shoot with a deer hanging over his shoulder. Unaware of the permission Harry had been given, he immediately instructed him to drop it and told him he was on a charge for poaching. Harry said nothing, rather enjoying what he knew would be the outcome of this little encounter. Ordered before the CO, Harry's crime was read out by the bristling RSM. The colonel sat, saying nothing. Let Harry continue:

> Then he leaned back and said to the RSM, 'Do you not know who this man is? He's my sniper sergeant and if he can't shoot deer, I don't know who can, besides he has my special permission to do so. Now go away and don't waste my time like this again.' He then had the grace to apologise to me and told me to collect a chit from HQ office, which he would sign, to prevent anything like it happening again.

Harry remained very much a rifleman during his time in Germany and aside from hunting deer, his appointment as Weapons Training Sergeant enabled him to compete in regimental shooting events, which he loved. He was again detailed to work closely with Captain Simmil, whom he admired greatly. The captain realised that Harry's shooting skills were quite exceptional and he was promptly made captain of the regimental shooting team. They went on to become shooting champions in several army competitions, a fact Harry was justifiably proud of.

> We out-shot all competitors at the inter-brigade championships held at the huge former German Army ranges called Haltern, which we renamed 'BIG' (Bisley In Germany). After the event, which every unit in the occupying army competed in, a General Officer awarded us the champions shield for all-round abilities, using every known infantry weapon, and plus that success I was fortunate enough to win outright three further individual shooting championships, which included the all-comers' sniper competition, open to all Allied snipers still stationed in Germany.

This very modest comment actually belied Harry's achievement, for in winning the individual competition he had out-shot *every* sniper and marksman in the British and Canadian occupation armies, which was no mean feat as the competition was, as he put it 'gruelling'. It was a three-day event shot at varying ranges, at daybreak, daytime and twilight and also required that competitors fired every infantry weapon, from revolvers to Bren guns, so merely being accurate with a rifle was not enough. The Regimental Museum of the Yorks and Lancs at Rotherham still retains the divisional Inter-Brigade Challenge Shield.

Early in the occupation the Hallamshires were based in the village of Neheim Hüsten in Westphalia. Their battalion commander wanted to get to know the area better so exploratory patrols were still being sent out to reconnoitre. Harry and another sniper were keeping an eye on some wounded Germans when he saw something with his Scout telescope that literally stopped him in his tracks – a very pretty girl with a tumbling mass of dark hair hanging out washing in a garden. He cautiously made his way towards her and began a hesitant conversation in German.

She had just arrived as a refugee with her mother, and I reckon I can be accused of the worst chat-up line ever, for I asked her politely and smiling if she had anything I could eat? It turned out her name was Erni. Like every young soldier I was always hungry and my battalion was so far advanced we had actually run out of food supplies. They had fled in fear from their home in eastern Germany before the Red Army attacked the region, losing her father, brother and sister as well as everything they had ever owned. Erni and her mother had made their way towards Dresden where they had relatives and friends, they were almost in there when the allies firebombed the city, killing 50,000 tightly packed residents and refugees. As Dresden had been put forward as an 'Open City' of great cultural value (like Paris) the Germans didn't ring the city with protective anti-aircraft artillery and the only troops who remained … were the wounded in various hospitals. So, it was mine and her good fortune that Erni was still outside the city when the 1,000-bomber raids started. She had been caught in the street back home when it was strafed by fighters and also in a packed train with only refugees travelling away from the advancing front-lines, it was strafed end to end a few times by fighter planes.

Amazingly perhaps to today's generation, neither Erni nor Harry had had boy or girlfriends; he had been only sixteen when he joined the army and she had led quite a sheltered life as the daughter of a middle-class dentist. That she survived her perilous journey westwards through war-torn Germany was as remarkable as Harry's survival as a combat sniper. This meeting was to have happy unforeseen consequences, which will be explained later.

Nevertheless, the days of occupation passed slowly, with all of the men naturally anxious to get home and resume their civilian lives. But Harry was enjoying his time in Germany and had found to his surprise that he possessed a natural ability with languages, having taught himself to speak German. He was actually fluent enough to be considered bi-lingual, so this proved very useful when dealing with the locals, who suffered from minor depredations such as chickens that apparently laid no eggs and cows that mysteriously had no milk, but he also gained a lot of understanding about the attitude of the civilians to the war, to Hitler and to the more fanatical branches of the German military. Few had any time for them and Harry was always impressed at how courteous and open the residents were to the occupying army. It also made his blossoming relationship with Erni far easier.

One other notable event occurred during this period:

> In the summer of 1945 two Army Film and Photographic Unit soldiers turned up, an officer who did the interview and a sergeant/cameraman. [They] came to Arnsberg in Westphalia, and took some photographs of me for a series they had started about soldiers who had distinguished themselves in some way during the campaign across North-West Europe. Over the years that particular photograph has been published in several military books.

Harry's relationship with Erni was also going from strength to strength and he realised that, in his words, 'We were made for each other.' The obvious outcome of this was that he proposed and she duly accepted. It may seem this topic is miles away from the gritty story of a combat sniper but war is all about people, soldiers and civilians alike, and the suffering that both endured. Harry's story and later life were inextricably intertwined with that of Erni and, as he pointed out, if it had not been for the war and the fact that he was a sniper, they would simply never have met. He decided to ask permission from Lt.-Colonel Halford to marry, a simple enough request one would think, but it put the occupying authorities into a flat spin, for he seems to have been the first Allied soldier who asked to marry a former enemy national.

> It was sometime in late 1945 that we attempted our first application to see if marriage would be permitted, but it was far too early for the authorities to consider, so it was not accepted at the time. In early 1946 we were officially engaged under German conventions, with parents on both sides in full agreement. After this we were busy collecting together all the very many relevant documents needed

Aftermath and Later Life

to obtain permission to marry. This was extremely taxing for Erni, who had lost everything. There was very much confusion at the time over what type of paperwork we might need ... so we slogged on so that eventually we had a very thick file to satisfy all parties.

Around the time of my birthday, 10 March 1947, my commanding officer told me he had been ordered to send me to Army HQ as a very senior officer wanted to talk to me. As a young sergeant I admit I was overawed at the prospect of a high-ranking officer wanting to see me for I assumed it would be a high-level discouragement discussion, but it wasn't like that at all. I travelled to Hamburg Hauptbahnhof where an army driver picked me up for my appointment with a brigadier and his aide. The brigadier was courteous to me, almost fatherly in fact. He was well informed of my previous application to marry, and he knew that I'd been photographed by the AFPU and I'm sure that helped my application request.

I do remember it was a long discussion. He wanted to know how I had met my German fiancée and how fluent I was in German ... whereupon in view of my interest in languages, he kindly offered to post me to a London school to study Japanese! He told me that Japanese linguists were needed in the Far East (where heavy fighting was still continuing),[1] I very politely declined this fine offer as I wished to remain with my regiment until demobilised.

He gave me a wise assessment of the resentment we could face following a major war and he was right about that, as we eventually found. But before I left his office, he told me that he hoped my bride-to-be and I would have a long and happy life together, so I knew right away that he was going to approve my marriage request ...

That decisive interview ... gave my Commanding Officer just sufficient time to rush though planning details for our marriage so the ceremony could take place before the battalion entrained for new duties in Berlin. The troop train was scheduled to leave early on 23 March 1947. It was packed solid with soldiers and supplies, but even so the regimental officers of my battalion had done us proud, for they had arranged for us a separate compartment garlanded with flowers with a large notice 'Reserved for Sergeant and Mrs Furness'.

During that immediate post-war period, I held the appointment of Regimental Intelligence Sergeant and remained so until I left Berlin for final demobilisation. On our arrival in Berlin, we stayed at first in a small hotel in the Reichstrasse ... but soon moved into an apartment near our barracks in Berlin-Spandau.

Someone must have alerted the German news media that the very first marriage was to take place between an English–German couple in Lüneberg [sic],[2] because they were waiting outside the church of St Nicholas as we newly-weds came out. Amongst them was the photojournalist Josef Makovec ... in later years he became famous in his profession for magazine reportage.

My commanding officer was gracious enough to loan me his personal Jeep for my wife and I for the trip to church, and rather curiously we were also loaned a BGC with driver to transport our few wedding guests, mostly my bride's relatives. It was a thoughtful kindness I never forgot ... we fought together and had a lot of respect for each other. I must add that the military authorities can move very fast sometimes. By early April 1947 I had already received a communication from the ... UK that my army pay had been increased as a married senior NCO, plus back-dated!

Return to Civilian Life

As Intelligence Sergeant for the rest of his time in Germany Harry was sufficiently highly thought of by his superiors to be offered further promotion if he signed on again for another term in the army. But he had had enough, both mentally and physically, and wanted to return to a civilian occupation, although at the time he had absolutely no idea of what that might prove to be. He was ordered to return to Britain at the end of 1947 and did so with a slight twist in the tale.

> Of course, when you are demobbed, you return only with your ordinary kit, except for weapons and specialised items, which you have to hand over to the RQMS, and these have to be signed for. I was still in possession of my number two rifle, of course, so I duly handed over my faithful No. 4 (T), my telescope etc., packed my kit, put my other rifle in its slip-case and climbed into a lorry to take us to the station, as we were not being flown back. When I finally arrived in England, we had to pass through a security area staffed by Military Police, who would search anyone they thought was suspicious. I was a sergeant sniping instructor of course, and when they asked where I was going with my rifle, I simply said 'Sniper Training Establishment' which was true, and that was that. I left carrying my rifle, went home and dropped it off, then a day or so later reported to Warminster.

Harry and his 'No. 2' sniping rifle were to have many more years of shooting together as he subsequently legally registered it in Britain and used it in competitive target meetings until 1983, when he began to find the vision in his 'good' right eye was also deteriorating.

> I put this down to countless hours of looking through the Scout Regiment telescope, which was very hard on the eyes. It was interesting that Major Hesketh-Prichard (the Great War exponent of all things sniping) also suffered from the same problem, eventually becoming almost blind in that eye. My left eye was also a problem because of the wounds but there was little that could be done medically then, and I was advised that not straining my eyes was the best thing I could do.

He was very loath to part with his beloved rifle, though, and this led to an amusing encounter many years later with the Administration Office at the School of Infantry at Warminster, then also housing the Army School of Sniping. He telephoned a corporal, explaining that he would like to have the rifle de-activated, so he could keep it without requiring a firearms certificate. The corporal asked who he was, then explained that the army 'didn't do that sort of thing' and that he would have to take it to a firearms dealer. There was a pause on the line as someone spoke to the corporal, then another voice came onto the phone, introducing himself as the Commanding Officer. He asked if he was speaking to '*The former Sniper Sergeant Harry Furness?*' which Harry confirmed. The major then made him an irresistible offer: 'If you would be prepared to come down as our guest for a day and perhaps give us a lecture on your experiences, I'm sure we could manage to put the rifle through our workshops for you.' This was duly arranged, and Harry was treated with great kindness as an honoured guest for the day. His rifle was totally refurbished (though sadly losing all its wartime patina in the process), and legally de-activated. Harry retained it until only a few years before he died.

Harry still refused all enticements to re-enlist, and he was officially demobilised in January 1948. This meant he had to decide on what he subsequently wanted to do for a living. His sole qualification was that of sniper, and he did appreciate that it was a trade that was not in great demand in peacetime Britain. Meanwhile Erni had flown over to join him, having finally been issued with her new British passport. Like thousands of others, Harry was now an unemployed former soldier, with no professional qualifications or even a place to live. For a while he stayed with his parents in their tiny house, but as he said:

> Although we liked each other very much, it was too crowded and I wanted my own place as soon as possible. So I bought a showman's travelling caravan which I sited wherever was convenient until I could sort out a house for us. Whatever I had of value was sold, poignant memories or not. Battle stress symptoms really only surfaced much later; that is common, I'm told.

In the summer of 1950, Harry was very alarmed to be warned that, as he was still in the army reserve as a sniper, he might well be recalled and sent to Korea, where war had just broken out.

> This was not news I was expecting, or wanted. I had had enough of sniping and the army and just wanted to make a peaceful life for ourselves. It worried me considerably for

quite some time until I was informed that the army had decided that any former soldier who had been previously wounded would not be recalled to the colours. So, much to my relief, I was 'off the hook'.

Inevitably, Erni was homesick at various times; post-war Britain was not exactly full of forgiving people and understandably she suffered from considerable verbal abuse from those who had lost relatives, livelihoods or homes in the war. Harry felt that there were actually more opportunities in Germany than England, and at one point they were seriously considering if moving back was perhaps the best option. They went so far as to return to look at different areas and available housing, and there seemed to be no difficulties in their obtaining German residency. However, the deciding factor was their young daughter Annette, who was now of school age and was doing so well that they felt it would be wrong to disrupt her studies. Besides, by this time Erni was working for the Bayer Company in Cheshire, quite near to where they had bought a small house. Bayer was an excellent employer and Erni's bi-lingual skills were very useful so, as the family seemed settled, they decided that Erni's mother should come to live with them. Tragedy was to strike, though, as just before she was due to leave Germany, she fell down a flight of stone steps, injuring herself fatally.

What Harry did in the 1950s and early 60s is unclear, and was even to Harry in later life: he said that for a time he was 'bewildered as to where his future lay'. He did many and varied odd jobs, including some shop work. He became the manager of an antique shop named Henderson and White, where he increased his knowledge of, and liking for antique furniture and especially long-case clocks. So too did one of his customers, a gentle-mannered artist named L. S. Lowry, who purchased many items from him.

Exactly what prompted Harry to move on to photography is unknown, but from his earlier comments about captured German cameras he obviously already possessed some interest and knowledge of the subject. He loved the technical side of cameras, and the processes involved in making prints. Erni had given him a service manual on Leicas which she had found in Berlin so this may well have been the catalyst that prompted him into turning an interest into a career, mating with his artistic streak and leading him to take up photography. He began as a general high-street photographer, which he did not particularly enjoy, then moved to more specialist business and industrial photography and his professional career went from strength to strength. He became the European Photographer for International News Photos, based in New York, whose British offices were in Fleet Street, London. Fortunately, Harry lived close to Manchester Airport from where he regularly took flights to anywhere in Europe that his services were needed.

> I never considered general work, so I also spent some time specialising for various offices in what you might call loosely 'Industrial Information'. I was always in and out of research centres, test stations, scientific laboratories, visiting inventors, anyone who was designing or even had an interesting prototype anywhere and I might be found nearby. I spent a lot of time travelling all the continental countries, I was at all the major international trade fairs and symposiums seeking out boffins, new types of machinery electronics ... even visiting oil rigs. I worked on many assignments for British government departments ... it was far from being easy work, it was stressful and I worked the clock around; when I arrived home (sometimes weeks later) I was thinner and had black circles under my eyes.
>
> I took my main orders straight from the INP head offices in New York. Perhaps it may seem strange but at the time I was also chief photographer of the Manchester-based Press Agency, which also ran other agencies in the region such as the GNS, LPA, YPA, MPA and TTNS.[3] It typically meant long weeks, seventy hours being usual. Not surprisingly, this led to my first heart attack! Afterwards, I changed my coverage from press to the less stressful magazine work.
>
> I used many types of equipment, from Minox ultra-miniature ... right up to 7×5-inch. My most used gear, however, were Leicas, mostly special black-painted press models. I had a special Press Model Leica fitted with a 21mm lens, which allowed me to photograph military

A picture taken in the late 1950s, Harry holding the Leica that he used to provide many high-quality images for the American International News Photos wire-service. He pointed out that the strain of his new job was already visible on his face.

manoeuvres for the MoD, including mass parachute drops. I also used a Nikon F that was fitted with a rare Remopak motor-drive. Sometimes a big 5×4-inch Pacemaker Speed Graphic was useful, but it wasn't exactly portable! The very nature of my work has caused some to assume it was something other than it really was, mainly because of my close connection with the Central Office of Information – that's their error though!

Never one to do anything by halves, Harry became a Fellow of the Royal Photographic Society, Associate of the Institute of Incorporated Photographers, Fellow of the Royal Society of Arts and member of the Master Photographers' Association. He covered several royal visits to the north-east, and remembered with a big grin the time he was climbing a ladder to take some photographs of the Queen. The strain was too much for his trousers, which promptly split, causing Her Majesty to burst out laughing. His career was to prove very successful and he loved it, but admitted he was glad to be able to retire; he had two heart attacks as a result of the workload and as he aged the physical and mental demands of his wartime service began to take their toll. His war injuries did not leave him unscathed, for all those months of stress and poor diet, allied to heavy daily physical demands, were not something that many human bodies would recover from entirely.

It is hard not to think that, compared to the years in trenches that his father's generation experienced, then surely Harry and the other Allied soldiers fighting in North-West Europe for less than a year could not have suffered that badly. But, when examined closely, the facts tell a different story.

In the course of one year, the average British soldier during the First World War would have served 60–70 days in the front-line trenches, only half of which would have been in the actual firing line, the balance in reserve or support trenches. If no major offensive was under way, many would not even fire their rifles in anger during all that time. They were surrounded by comrades and, as one Great War veteran told the author, his service 'Was 90 per cent boredom and 10 per cent terror.' The rest of their service would have been out of the front lines completely, although admittedly sometimes this was also within range of enemy artillery.

On the other hand, from D-Day onwards, Harry served *continuously* for almost a year, with only three weeks of proper rest completely out of the lines. He was also a sniper, without doubt the most physically and mentally demanding high-risk specialist profession in the army, and worked for most of the time on his own. He needed to be cautious almost to the point of obsession, and had to adjust to the physical and mental strains resulting from having been twice wounded. So it was unsurprising that he returned home with a stomach ulcer, shell-splinter wounds that had not healed properly, hearing loss and damaged eyesight, which continued to deteriorate. Physically, like thousands of other veterans, he continued to pay for his war for the rest of his life.

Chapter 7

Reflections

I ASKED HARRY, with the hindsight of seventy years, what were his thoughts about his unique profession and how it affected him in his later life? There was no question in his mind about the validity of what his profession entailed.

> Snipers provide a veil of protection for our troops against enemy snipers … enemy snipers will always be out there. Without our snipers to handle them many on our side would have died. It is impossible to assess exactly how many very-high-ranking combat soldiers are still around today because their lives were saved from enemy sniper fire by the actions of our own snipers … what would happen if our snipers were not there? I know I saved very many lives. You always had to be one step ahead of the game and I am often minded of the comment by the late W. C. Fields as he selected a new victim for a game of cards. When asked 'Is this a game of chance?' Fields replied 'Not the way I play it.'

As to the sort of soldier he was during the war, he had clearly thought about it a great deal in the intervening years.

> How was I earlier? … I can't explain easily. One old former soldier said … I was a 'cold blooded little devil' and another called me a 'small evil sod'. When I heard what they said about me, well it just tickled my funny bone and I laughed, only Erni commented it wasn't very flattering! Were they right? I have to accept their opinions as valid from their viewpoint … but it was the *only* way I could have carried out my tasks at that time. I just 'switched off' all my inner emotions, just the same as every other sniper had to do. From my part, after a fierce firefight I used to look around

at the dead and although I felt hurt by the loss of good mates in the battalion, in looking at the enemy dead I had no feelings. I suppose it was an in-built protective measure that I lost all compassion, all pity ... I found I could 'switch-off' any inner feelings so I didn't think of them as someone's father, brother or sweetheart. Yet I did respect them for their bravery. Somehow it seemed unreal, but I felt no regrets as a soldier, nor pride in having helped another battle success, I realised only that I was glad to have survived another day. I always carried out my duties efficiently and with great reliability, but I wasn't able to mix; as a loner I was never 'one of the lads'. At least they gave me a great reference when I left the army. I began to suffer from intense nightly sweats. No flash-backs, nothing melodramatic, just not too well. Quite obviously all that stress which I never allowed to show (like every infantry soldier in constant fighting) then ... piled up inside me and slowed me down in later life. But it takes time to adjust and once I was able to accept it was all behind me, then I slowly changed. Erni had witnessed first-hand what war was really like, so her understanding made all the difference.

I have changed. Partly this is due to increasing age, becoming more mellow [with] a strong desire to make up for past actions I told myself were necessary at that grim period. Memories of my sniping missions now jumble together as so much happened ... My bitter experiences left me with deeply embedded memories which have taken years to dim. Though I was intensely grateful to survive the fighting, in a curious way I also felt a sense of guilt that I remained alive, when so many of my army mates didn't make it through ... snipers in particular. The average life expectancy of a sniper in Normandy was about three weeks, I believe, about the same as a subaltern on the Somme in 1916. New replacements would arrive, go out and then simply never come back. You never knew if they were dead or captured. After the ceasefire in 1945 and POWs were released, our battalion did get to hear what had happened to many we hadn't been able to account for ...

but not a single sniper ever returned from a POW camp, so we drew the inescapable conclusion.

In my conversations with him over the years, it was clear that, as he aged, what he had done in the past bothered him. This is an attitude, I might add, that is common to every sniper I have ever interviewed, all of whom in older age began to have more time for troubled reflection on their past lives. Many developed alcohol-related problems as a result. Harry was of sterner stuff, and knew that his job was utterly necessary and saving British lives brought him some solace but, even so, he was clearly uncomfortable about his past.

> My memories of my time with Erni are a joy to me, but not my memories of war as a sniper. I haven't the words to describe the sheer horror of fighting as a sniper in Normandy.

Quite out of the blue, in 2017, Harry was contacted by the French Embassy in London to inform him he had been awarded the Légion d'Honneur for his services in liberating France after D-Day. In his quiet way, this belated recognition of what he and so many others had done pleased him greatly. The fact is that he became, and will always remain, Britain's highest-scoring sniper of the Second World War, albeit this was a statistic that he took absolutely no pleasure in. In February 2020, after 73 years of marriage, his beloved Erni died, aged 93. Harry was bereft and he passed away in March the following year, just short of his ninety-seventh birthday. Today they are still together as they always were, in a quiet cemetery in Weston-super-Mare. On the headstone beneath their names is engraved:

A True WWII Love Story

Appendix 1

The Enfield No. 4 (T) Sniping Rifle

A Development History

This is a brief overview of how arguably the most iconic sniping rifle of the twentieth century came into being. It includes the most significant technical developments but is by no means meant to be an exhaustive study of the subject. For those interested in learning more, various authoritative books listed in the bibliography cover the model's history in far greater detail.

The Enfield family of military rifles had a long and distinguished history, dating back to the first Pattern 1853 rifled musket. They were made to exacting standards, with Victorian craftsmanship allied to the latest mass-production techniques. They were state-of-the art and set a new benchmark for British military long arms. However, the introduction in 1889 of the Magazine, Lee-Metford Mk I was a giant technological leap forward. It was a new type of high-velocity, magazine-fed, bolt-action rifle and it brought Britain's armed forces into the era of modern centrefire weapons. In 1902 the Short, Magazine Lee-Enfield Mk I was introduced, evolving by 1907 to become the Enfield No. 1 Mk III, the much-loved SMLE, or 'Smellie'. It was a world first, having been introduced as a practical compromise between the shorter carbines required by mounted troops and artillerymen and the long rifles carried by infantry, which had meant that until then armies had to supply two different patterns of rifle.

Despite considerable opposition at the time, it was to become an excellent firearm, perhaps the best combat rifle used in the First World War. When hastily modified as a sniping rifle, however, it showed up certain deficiencies – mainly because it was never designed with sniping in mind. Indeed, the whole concept was alien to the British Army until mounting losses in the trenches due to German sniping required a rapid solution to be found.

This was done on an *ad hoc* basis, with a bewildering number of telescopic sights and mounts being fitted to SMLEs. These can be distilled down to three major types: Periscopic Prism scopes and mounts, Aldis Brothers scopes of various patterns and American Winchester A5 telescopes were the most numerous. This was a half-hearted response, though, for the rifle was not especially accurate, the telescopes were under-powered and the bizarre insistence by the Army that all of the scope mounts were to be offset to the left (to permit charger-loading) was baffling. This offset effectively prevented the proper use of loopholes in steel sniping plates, as the aperture blocked the view from the scope at any extreme angles. A solution was belatedly found, in the shape of the Pattern 1914 Mk 1*W (T) rifle, with its strong Mauser-actioned bolt design, excellent micro-adjustable iron sights and a telescopic sighting system unashamedly copied from a German Hensoldt type. The scope was mounted centrally over the bore of the rifle and would have proven ideal were it not for the fact it was only accepted for service in December 1918, a month after the Armistice.

The problem with all British sniping rifles was that there had never been any single, pre-determined pattern approved for issue. In fact, the multitude of combinations of scopes and mounts proved a logistical nightmare for stores and armourers to keep and maintain in working condition, not helped by the fact that many had been manufactured in very small numbers, so it was simply common sense to replace all of them with a single pattern, properly tested and approved by the Small Arms Committee (SAC). Thus, to the sorrow of many latter-day collectors, in 1923 the SAC instructed that all reserves of SMLE sniping rifles held in military stores were to be decommissioned. Some of the excellent Aldis pattern scopes as well as stored P. 1914 (T) rifles were set aside for possible future use, but the vast majority of telescopic sights were stripped from their rifles, to be sold off to the gun trade where they were refurbished and mostly fitted to sporting rifles.

In what direction this planned re-arming of the British Army might be heading was entirely open to conjecture, but one unexpected lesson from the Great War was that even with maximised wartime production, the RSAF at Enfield took 72 hours to fabricate a rifle. Despite an impressive total wartime output in excess of 5,000,000 rifles, this still proved to be insufficient. Quite simply, British manufacturers could not keep pace with the demand for replacement rifles during a major conflict. Tens of thousands were lost due to enemy action, and any salvaged ones took an inordinate amount of time to repair. In peacetime such production figures were utterly unachievable and this had to be borne in mind in any future decision-making. Whatever was decided upon had to be faster and simpler to manufacture as well as performing as both an infantry rifle and a highly accurate sniping rifle. This was a tall order.

Neither was the process of deciding on a new rifle a simple one. In 1921 the SAC had convened to determine what route should be taken regarding the future of the SMLE, both as an infantry and as a sniping rifle. The reality was that it was no longer satisfactory. But there was no new type of rifle available that could be produced in the very large numbers required and was as tough and reliable as the SMLE, yet more accurate, more cost-efficient and easier to manufacture.

Of course, one possibility was to look again at the Pattern 1914 rifle. It had been designed pre-war to accept the radical new high-velocity Pedersen .276 in. rimless cartridge, although wartime expediency meant the rifles were chambered only for .303 in. or US .30-06 in. ammunition. What had to be considered, too, was the high cost of re-equipping the dozens of ammunition plants to produce a .276 in. cartridge, which would be utterly prohibitive. (Britain had manufactured some 6 billion .303 in. cartridges during 1914–18.) There were also time-consuming technical problems yet to be ironed out with the new ammunition and a further disadvantage was that existing .303 in. barrels could not be cost-effectively relined or reamed out to accept its rimless case design. This meant that brand-new barrels would need to be produced. Although the P. 14 was known to be both accurate and reliable it required expensive new tooling to begin manufacture in quantity. Besides, it used a harder-to-obtain one-piece stock with a butt that could not be changed, as was possible on the SMLE; the Mauser-type bolt and receiver were more difficult to machine; and the magazine held only five cartridges. By 1930 the hoped-for overhaul of small arms had also grown to encompass the possibility of adopting more semi-automatic and automatic weapons, one of which was the Bren Light Machine Gun. The overriding problem facing the government was that there was virtually no money in the Exchequer to begin producing *any* new weapon.

So, the most sensible compromise appeared to be to undertake a re-design of the SMLE to lower manufacturing costs, and upgrade it to make it more accurate. This meant that it would be possible to retain the tried and tested .303 in. cartridge, albeit with its rather outmoded tapered, rimmed cartridge case, as well as most of the extant manufacturing facilities, and this actually proved to be a very wise decision in the face of future events. Thus, many of the .303 in. Great War-vintage weapons such as the Vickers Medium Machine Gun, Lewis Light Machine Gun and newer developments like the Bren Gun, were all designed to be chambered for the old cartridge.

Work was actually begun in 1922 to design a replacement infantry rifle that was initially designated the No. 1 Mk V. This actually bore a close resemblance to the original Enfield No. 1 Mk III. It had much improved iron sights, with a rear- to front-sight distance that was double that of the old SMLE: the rear sight was now much closer to the shooter's eye and a fixed-aperture battle sight on it provided an immediate sight picture out to 200 yards. The nose-cap was retained to allow use of the long (but by then, largely redundant) Pattern 1907 sword bayonet and a two-piece wooden handguard was fitted from the muzzle to the receiver. This was a half-measure, though, as crucially the cost of producing the 20,000 trials rifles made in 1922–24 turned out to be about 15 per cent more than the old SMLEs!

This work was undertaken by the RSAF at Enfield, who reworked these 'A' series prototypes and then quickly produced a modified 'B' Series, designated the No. 1, Mk VI, manufactured as 1,000 prototype rifles in 1930–31. A quick glance shows that these are clearly still hybrids, with the two-piece stock, new sights, heavily chequered fore-end and rounded cocking piece of the old SMLE.

Finally, though, they lost their distinctive snub-nosed appearance with the replacement of the nose cap by a protruding muzzle on which a lug was machined to enable a small spike bayonet to be attached. The single Enfield rear-locking lug of the bolt was still retained in preference over the double locking system of the Mauser, as it was faster to make and arguably just as strong, but the new receiver was of a more square design, far easier for machining operations although the right side of the receiver was still, rather oddly, slotted to accept the redundant magazine cut-off feature of the SMLEs. Eventually this was omitted altogether when the first production No. 4 rifles were produced.

From the point of view of producing a sniping variant, the most critical change was the introduction of a 'floating barrel' which was designed to sit inside the fore-end woodwork without touching it at any point. This was a well-understood modification made on all very accurate target rifles and it prevented rain-soaked wood from swelling and pressing on the barrel, as was the case with the SMLE. This slight pressure prevented the barrel from retaining its natural harmonics when it vibrated with each shot. (Think in terms of pressing a finger lightly on a humming tuning fork, the process is the same.) Allowing a barrel to resonate at exactly the same frequency with every shot actually mattered little under normal battle conditions, where shooting any further than 300 yards was rare.[1] But for sniping it was a crucial factor in ensuring a rifle worked at its optimum accuracy *every* time it was fired, which was an absolute pre-requisite.

Some 2,479 of these rifles, designated the No. 4 Mk I, were produced in 1931–34 and were issued for testing to the Hythe School of Musketry from mid-1932 onwards, although a very few 1935-dated examples have also surfaced. Many were actually produced as production-run tests to see how the new tooling performed and to keep the RSAF artificers working.

Troop trials were started in 1935 when the instructors at Hythe tested twelve SMLE No. 1 Mk III rifles against twelve new Mk 4s, which proved informative. The No. 4s were all more accurate in 'rapid fire, snap-shooting, and fire with movement' by quite a margin, depending on each individual rifle (and these were off-

Harry's No. 2 rifle, with the scope serial number '9369' on the top of the stock wrist. The curve where the base of the rear sight has been ground away can be seen, enabling the bolt to be removed with the scope in situ. The bolt handle has the rifle serial number stamped on it. There is no Holland and Holland 'S51' code stamped underneath the stock wrist, as Harry had his stocks changed for a short pattern in the field.

the-production-line weapons, not specially selected), of between 2 per cent and 20 per cent. In particular, the fine adjustable aperture sight was rated very highly. Post-trials, these rifles were marked with an 'A' suffix before their serial numbers to indicate that they contained parts and tolerances that were not factory-standard. After the war these were mostly removed from army stores as they posed a problem for repair or spares and are understandably extremely rare today.

The No. 4 Mk I Rifle

As Britain drifted inexorably towards another European war in the late 1930s, so the requirement for a new rifle became more urgent and the No. 4 Mk I was accepted to be mass-produced as the new infantry rifle, and approved for service in November 1939. Immediate production of large numbers was something of a problem, however, for the RSAF was already heavily engaged in making machine guns and pistols, so two new Royal Ordnance Factories were established, one at Maltby near Sheffield and another at Fazakerley near Liverpool. Birmingham Small Arms (BSA) was already well established in Small Heath but also set up a second factory in Shirley, Solihull. Other facilities were established abroad, in America, Canada and India. Production began in mid-1940 at Maltby, a year later at Fazakerley. BSA suffered very heavy bomb damage in 1940, which dramatically slowed down its output but by 1941 all of the factories in the UK and North America were in full production.

The No. 4 rifle was thus on its way to becoming Britain's new standard infantry long-arm, being first issued in 1941 and going through a number of improvements during its service life. But what of the requirement for a new sniping rifle? The 1925 SAC recommendations on the introduction of a new sniping weapon had been borne in mind during the long gestation of the No. 4, but there were many problems inherent in actually setting up a facility to manufacture useful quantities of production military rifles to a sniping standard. The biggest issue was how to convert these to sniping configuration, because although RSAF Enfield had produced the first batch of trials No. 4 (T)s, they simply did not have the capacity to undertake the work in any quantity. So an agreement was reached whereby examples of production-line rifles from the BSA and Maltby factories[2] that had performed particularly well in test-firing would be passed to the well-respected London gunmaker Holland & Holland as it had the capacity and skills to produce what were effectively custom-built rifles, but on a large scale. Eventually it appears that only BSA-manufactured rifles proved consistently accurate enough to be selected. Exactly what percentage were chosen from production numbers is unknown, but one well-informed estimate believes it was no more than 1 per cent.

The Holland & Holland Conversions

Holland & Holland (H&H) was in some ways fortunate that the war had effectively put a stop to their peacetime production of quality sporting rifles. Most of its customers were now in the armed forces or preoccupied by greater matters than stalking game. This had led to the many skilled gunsmiths in London, Birmingham and other areas becoming absorbed into a small elite of highly qualified workers who could be employed in specialist weapons production. As a pre-war company, H&H could not possibly have taken on the task of building sniping rifles on such a scale unless it could be expanded to meet the demands of the army. As it was, they were very fortuitously able to recruit all the redundant gunsmiths they needed, who were only too willing to do what they were best at, producing highly accurate rifles.

The selected No. 4 rifles were set aside at the factory, but this was an unpredictable process. This explains why today there are no blocks of serial numbers that can be said to have been specifically allocated to sniping rifles. From the summer of 1942, H&H was scheduled to handle all of the conversion work and it began matching rifles to No. 32 Mk I scopes. From this date the factory gradually began to introduce a marking system on components that showed they had passed through the required production and inspection procedures and that the rifle actions were fitted with the correct barrels and iron sights. The work that needed to be done to each Enfield was considerable, as each was first stripped until only the barrel and receiver remained together. All the wooden components were marked and kept together, as it was this unique combination of parts on every rifle that when assembled made it an exceptionally accurate weapon.

Although originally these standard production rifles were mostly (but not exclusively) fitted with two-groove, left-hand twist barrels, accuracy tests appeared to show that five-groove barrels were more accurate, although they were slightly more expensive because of the more complex manufacturing process. It was thus decided that, to enable the sniping variants to be as uniform and accurate as possible, a five-groove should be fitted as standard.[3] Experience in World War One and through years of civilian target shooting had also shown that accuracy was also improved by fitting thicker-walled barrels, which are inherently more rigid, whereas bedding was a preferred solution for thinner barrels. There had to be some compromise in wartime production, however, as special thick target barrels were more expensive as well as heavier and could not be fitted economically to mass-produced rifles. Whilst the production No. 4 had did have a slightly thicker barrel than the SMLE, bedding was the preferred means of fine-tuning them.

Universal fitting of five-groove barrels was the theory, but in practice it does not appear to have been quite so straightforward. Instructions were indeed issued that No. 4 (T) models should not be manufactured with two-groove barrels, but in practice this does not always appear to have been the case. Sometimes the exigencies of supply meant that what was available had to be used and doubtless to keep up production numbers some two-groove barrels were permitted. Thus, there still exist today original, untouched sniping rifles manufactured by Savage and Maltby with two-groove barrels which were converted by H&H without the specified barrel change.

Once the rifle had been completely stripped by the gunsmith the receiver was mounted in a jig and the left side machined perfectly flat, a crucial operation that enabled the fitting of two metal pads to it using solder with three securing screws on the front, two on the rear. The threaded screw holes for these pads had to be machined in the receiver wall at near-zero tolerance to ensure the pads fitted perfectly in place and the holes lined up when the mounting clamps of the scope were screwed onto these pads. The heavy scope and mount placed a considerable strain on the screws due to the recoil when fired, resulting in these small screws often working loose, so unit armourers used a centre-punch to 'stake' the edges of the screws to prevent them undoing themselves. A barrel then had to be carefully bedded in by the gunsmith, leaving it free-floating. The process used a traditional gunmakers' method of 'sooting up' the barrel and receiver over a smoky flame, fitting it into the stock and then examining it closely to see where the wood had taken on any black colour from touching the metalwork. This would then be shaped and filed until there were no traces of surface contact. The receiver and barrel were then replaced in the stock and screwed into position and the process repeated until the gunsmith or armourer was absolutely certain that it was perfectly bedded.

There was a small problem on these sniping variants due to a design oversight: it was not possible for the sniper to remove the bolt because the underneath of the rear sight fouled it. This (as Harry mentions) made cleaning a problem as it required the scope to be dismounted, an operation no sniper ever liked to do unless it was absolutely necessary. Whilst in theory the scope could be refitted without the loss of zero, in practice this seldom proved to be the case. Unit armourers solved the problem by filing a shallow groove in the lower body of the sight and this provided sufficient clearance to permit bolt removal. This became a standard practice on all later No. 4 (T) rifles.

The scope brackets were manufactured either by Rose Brothers (marked 'JC' or 'KD') or Dalgleish and Sons (sometimes found marked 'N92'). Because the half-rings holding the scope into its bracket could be accidentally swopped over, unwittingly fractionally altering its zero, they were stamped numerically as pairs so no error should occur. The scope was then perfectly collimated to the barrel and every completed rifle was test-fired at Holland's own ranges and small adjustments made to ensure trigger pull was smooth and consistent. The standard factory trigger was retained but the polishing work done by the gunsmiths meant that it proved to be a very smooth and progressive action, exactly what was required for accurate shooting. The usual set-up for the trigger was: first trigger

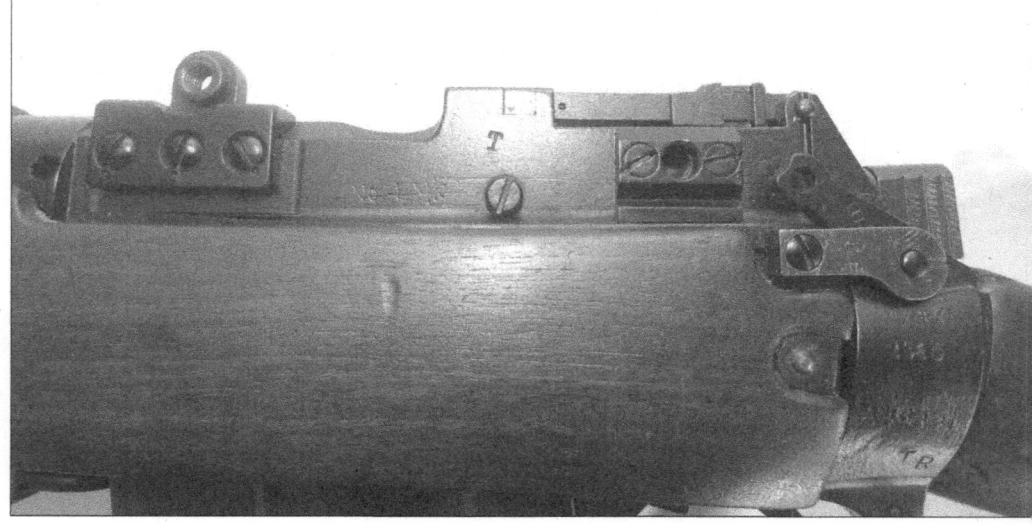

The scope bracket pads and mounting points on Harry's No. 2 rifle. The centre-punch marks on the five screw heads were standard procedure by late 1944. The rifle model 'No. 4 Mk I' can be seen as well as the 'T' mark denoting a completed conversion to sniping configuration.

pull, 2.5–3.5 lb, second pull, 4.5–5.5 lb. Each rifle tested by Holland & Holland had to produce a minimum accuracy with seven shots at 200 yards of a 5-inch group. At 400 yards, six out of seven shots had to be within a 10-inch circle. In practice many rifles were able to surpass this with ease. For the first time on a military sniping rifle, a wooden cheek rest was fitted to the stock, to provide a proper 'cheek weld' and a comfortable head position for the sniper.

The telescope's serial number was then stamped into the wrist of the stock, just below the cocking piece. The butt socket holding the stock was stamped at the BSA factory with the 'TR' mark to denote the rifle was selected for telescopic conversion. All battle sights were ground off and the rear sight refitted, the forward flat on the right of the receiver was stamped with an 'S' to denote that its correct Mk I rear-sight was fitted. The 'T' stamp went on the left receiver side-wall just after the rifle designation. The stock fitted was of a standard medium length and was marked with a large 'S51' underneath, in front of the knuckle, which was H&H's maker's code. Finally, the magazine, which alone was interchangeable with any other No. 4 rifle, was added; these were most often marked 'M56' but there were many manufacturers and most were unmarked.

After final inspection, the accepted rifle with its matched scope was marked with a small 'T' after its serial number on the left wrist. Holland and Holland produced over 23,000 No. 4 (T) rifles during the war.

The No. 32 Telescopic Sight

Of the many supply deficiencies facing Britain at the start of the 1939–45 war one of the most serious shortages was the lack of high-quality optical glass. Unlike Germany or Soviet Russia, Britain had never been a major centre for the production of optical instruments and there was little naturally occurring quartz glass, so it had to be imported from Austria or Switzerland. What limited quantities that were available were already earmarked for naval or artillery gunsights, military binoculars and observation telescopes.

One saving grace was that there were still 1,403 of the 1930s trials rifles in store at RSAF, so these were selected to be converted to sniping configuration, although exactly what that was to be was as yet undefined. Although there was a small unit of armourers at RSAF Enfield whose job was to strip and overhaul these trials weapons, some official decision had to be made as to what pattern of optical sight was to be fitted and how production could be greatly expanded.

The selection of H&H to produce these rifles solved the manufacture issue, but not the telescope supply one. Several commercial makes were considered before it was belatedly realised that provision had already been made for a telescopic sight to be fitted to the new Bren Gun! This had been adopted only recently (1938) and was proving to be one of the finest light machine guns ever manufactured. It was extremely accurate as well, so much so that a simple straight-sighting device, the No. 32 scope had originally been designed during trials, with the object of providing it with enhanced accuracy. Mk I Brens were even manufactured with a mounting lug machined on the left of the receiver, but in the event no scopes were ever fitted to them, being regarded as superfluous on a machine gun. Scopes that had been manufactured[4] were languishing in Enfield's stores and were examined to see if they could be adapted for conversion to fit a rifle. With some modifications to the range and deflection drums, it was believed that these robust scopes would indeed be suitable for the No. 4. Purely as a stopgap measure in the interim, the scoped Pattern 1914 Mk I* (T) rifles still held in stores were also refurbished for issue.

The No. 32 Mk I Scope

Technically, this was light years ahead of its Great War predecessors, having fixed 3× magnification and two adjuster drums, each of which had click adjustment for range and deflection. The top drum was set for a single click to alter range in 50-yard increments from 100 yards and this equated to ½ a minute-of-angle (MOA), one MOA therefore representing one inch of impact adjustment at 100 yards. However, to adjust for lateral drift a drum scale marked '16–0–16' gave the sniper 16 minutes-of-angle adjustment left and right with each click representing 2 MOA increments at 100 yards, this adjustment at the time being considered as less critical than the one for range. The range drum was in the usual position on top of the scope body, but rather unusually the deflection drum was on the left side of the scope because the original design called for it being mounted on the Bren where the receiver and magazine would have blocked easy access to a right-hand turret. In practice, this proved to be a perfectly practical place as the sniper could retain his positioning with his right arm, while adjusting with his left hand. It is reasonable to assume that the RSAF design team soon realised that the time that would be wasted and the complexities of re-designing the layout were not worthwhile, particularly as tooling already existed for the manufacture of the scope bodies. In the event, this didn't seem ever to pose a problem for snipers, Harry never once mentioning that it proved awkward.

The Mk I was first introduced in early 1942. It had slightly offset turret-drums and a distinctive angled sliding brass eye-shade at the ocular end, theoretically to prevent the ingress of light. It was common for telescopic sights to have eye cups, but these were normally manufactured of leather or rubber for one very good reason. When fired, the heavy recoil slams the rifle backwards, which is not a problem if your eye is at least a couple of inches away from it. However, with the metal eye shade pulled back, it brought its curved upper edge perilously close to the shooter's eyebrow and many shooters (the author included) have suddenly found their vision obscured by blood. It isn't serious, but it is unpleasant. Many of these sunshades were removed by snipers and consigned to the nearest ditch.

One minor problem was the fixed position in which the scope was clamped within its mounts. This was not variable so it could not be slid forwards or backwards to adjust for eye-relief. This is the distance between the shooter's eye and the ocular lens, which had to be fairly precise (2–2½ in. on a No. 32) to provide a full field of view without any visual impairment, like vignetting, where the target appears to have a black ring around its edge, or image distortion. The snipers simply learned to work around this and adjust their shooting positions accordingly. The correct length of stock was also quite important to provide the required eye-relief so a standard-length 12-inch stock was normally factory fitted, but three sizes were available. Due to his small stature, Harry always asked the unit armourers to fit a short stock, but added that on occasions when he used a standard one for short periods, it did not make much difference.

The scope bodies were blackened for obvious reasons, but instead of applying the traditional hard enamel finish, the Mk Is were chemically blackened, a quicker and more cost-effective process, but one that had not been tried before on the thin steel bodies of telescopic sights. One problem soon became evident, which was the appearance of pitting on the body due to a fine rust forming in damp weather, requiring the scope to be constantly cleaned and lightly oiled. The brass front and rear fittings were black enamelled.

Every mark of No. 32 scope was fitted with a vertical post and cross-wire reticle. It was the most commonly used pattern on military sniping rifles, believed to provide the clearest target image and providing the sniper with a rough method of judging the size of a target (and thus range) through knowing the height of a man at given distances, when measured against the vertical post. The field of view with the 19 mm objective lens was a tolerably useful

9 degrees, providing sufficient angle of vision to track a moving target at most ranges. The narrower the field of view, the harder it was to follow anything that was not static, one of the perennial problems inherent in using more powerful telescopes.

The next problem to be solved was how to mount the scope solidly to the No. 4 rifle. The left side of the receiver was not high or thick enough to screw a substantial bracket directly onto it, so, after the receiver had been machined flat and the two steel pads fitted, a curved cast-iron bracket was screwed in place, using a pair of large flat-headed thumb-screws to attach it to the pads. It was a large piece of metal to attach to any rifle, the scope and mount adding 2 lb 3 oz to its weight, bringing its total up to a hefty 11 lb but the combination proved to be an extremely solid assembly. As Harry once commented dryly: 'If your rifle jammed you could always remove the scope and mount and beat a German to death with it.'

The positioning of the new scope was also a great improvement, as finally it was fitted over the axis of the bore, so the right eye could naturally be used for aiming, something not all snipers could do comfortably with the previous generation of left-offset scopes. Furthermore, it was mounted low on the rifle, only just above the action, which provided a comfortable angle for the firers' head and this was enhanced by the cheek-rest. Earlier sniping rifles had scopes that were often too high as well as being offset, requiring some form of pad (often a thick field dressing) to be taped onto the stock.

Zeroing the Mk I scope was not a straightforward task, however, for once the rifle and scope were adjusted to shoot to exactly the point of aim, it was necessary for the graticule lines on the drums to be re-set to zero so that any future adjustments could be correctly calculated and undertaken. Thus, if on a Mk I scope, it was zeroed at 300 yards (the preferred distance for most snipers) a target at 450 yards would require the range drum on a Mk I to be adjusted by an additional 150 yards, with a similar process applied to the deflection drum if required. Snipers knew through training exactly how many click-stops were required for any given range, but this system only worked properly if the zero graticule on the adjuster drum had been re-set to zero to provide a datum point.

This rather cumbersome procedure required a special Mk 1 adjuster tool comprised of a rotating barrel to hold the locking ring and an inner post that was pressed down onto the central inner lead screw. The outer barrel and inner drum rotated independently if adjustments were needed and it helped greatly if a second pair of hands was available to hold the outer drum steady. The tool was easily lost and generally thoroughly disliked by snipers. So, in mid-1943, another tool was devised that enabled one man to operate the adjusting drums. It was usually referred to as the 'key and tongs' and was certainly an improvement, though it still remained an awkward procedure. As the scopes began to wear internally and the tiny internal spring weakened then 'backlash' could happen (as Harry mentions) in which the crosshair failed to sit correctly at its selected height because the spring no longer had the strength to retain it in position. Thus snipers learned to over-adjust by one or two clicks, then bring the cross-hair back down to ensure the reticle was at its correct setting.

An oblong steel scope carry-case, the 'No. 8 Mk I' was issued with every rifle. To hold the sight firmly when in transit there were two large internal brass securing posts for attaching the scope mounting screws and a spring clamp was rivetted into the lid for the Mk I adjuster tool. Two steel brackets underneath enabled a leather carry-strap to be fitted. After considerable use, this often split or became water-soaked and some snipers adopted thin webbing Sten gun slings, which were normally easy to acquire. All scopes were issued with a leather lens cover that had to be kept oiled to ensure it remained flexible and to prevent verdigris from forming between it and the scope body, as the front locking ring and eye-shade were made of brass. However, this worked well and remained unchanged until the rifles, in their final incarnation as L42A1s, were eventually taken out of service in the mid-1980s.

The No. 32 Mk II Scope

The Mk II scope, introduced in April 1943, was mostly (but not exclusively) manufactured without the lens shade. Otherwise, it looked identical externally to the Mk I. Internally, however, the problems of wear in the adjuster mechanism and the resultant backlash were addressed with the use of a stronger design of backlash spring, which provided a more positive click-stop. It was Harry's favourite scope and he retained this type on both of his rifles. The lens quality was improved, providing a slightly sharper image. Where there was some noticeable re-working was in the action of the adjuster drums, as the range was no longer in 50-yard increments, each click now representing one MOA, or one inch at 100 yards. This also applied to the deflection drum, providing a more precise lateral adjustment, something that snipers had complained was a particular problem on the Mk Is.

The No. 32 Mk III Scope

This final model of the No. 32 scope was approved in October 1944, although supplies of them did not reach any snipers in Europe until the very end of the war and then only when fitted to new production rifles. The most visible change was that the two adjuster turrets were now opposite each other instead of being offset and the rust-pitting problem had finally been overcome. While it was technically identical to the Mk II, retaining the same power, reticle type and one MOA adjustment, there were two further improvements made. The first was internal waterproofing of the body to combat the ingress of moisture – such scopes had a large red 'W' stencilled on them on the right side. The other was the gradual introduction of bloomed lenses, to improve the light-gathering properties, particularly at 'sniper's light' of dawn and dusk, when a telescope can pick out detail that the human eye cannot. Scopes thus fitted were painted with a blue 'B' on the left of the body. And finally, the overly-complex range-adjusting mechanism was simplified with a new slip-ring and the turrets could now be adjusted using just the pointed end of a bullet to depress the drum's locking ring.

Iron or Back-Up Sights

These were the standard metal sights, using a blade-type foresight mounted into a split block at the muzzle and this arrangement was specified for No. 4 (T) rifles. It was originally protected from damage by a waisted foresight protector that rather beautifully mirrored the contour of the barrel. It was a completely unnecessary and quite time-consuming item to machine but one that harked back just a little to the days of fine craftsmanship, when things not only had to be right, but also look right. Later foresight blocks eschewed this nicety and were slab-sided. The blade could be moved laterally in the block by loosening off its retaining screw and sliding it in the required direction via a dovetail slot. The front sight-blades came in variable height increments of 0.015 in., although the availability of such fine adjustment was rarely of any consequence to the snipers. There was a folding rear leaf-sight with a fine adjuster screw that operated a vertically sliding aperture sight. This was graduated from 200 to 1,300 yards in 50-yard increments and each increment could be further fine-adjusted by four clicks, providing a very precise approximate 12-yard adjustment. However, the graticule lines for the range scale were specifically calculated for the standard Mk VII ball ammunition in use and did not provide accurate ranging for tracer, armour-piercing or the heavier ball Mk VIIIz cartridges, although for snipers, who always used a scope, this was seldom an issue, simply requiring re-zeroing of the rifle.

A Note to Collectors

Genuine No. 4 (T) rifles now fetch considerable sums of money and there now exist several specialist companies who reproduce well-made replica parts such as pads, mounts and even No. 32 scopes. For shooters who cannot afford an original, but want to put a shooting No. 4 (T) together, this is, of course, absolutely perfect.

But, as with any field of collecting where large sums of money are involved, this has resulted in fakes being sold into the marketplace by the unscrupulous. There are some very talented fakers who are capable of ageing and stamping-up a lot of these modern parts on ordinary No. 4 donor rifles. Being sure of what you are buying is something of a minefield, though, as the vast majority of original surviving No. 4 (T) rifles will have led very hard lives over the intervening eighty-odd years. Worn-out or damaged parts such as barrels, bolts or stocks will have been changed and without doubt several different patterns of scope will have been fitted over time. To muddy the waters further, when changes have been made officially many rifles *may* have been correctly re-marked, but many have not. An ex-RSAF armourer told the author that post-war, he had racks of No. 4 (T)s and his job was to remove all the scopes and mounts, which were then separated and went into separate bins. The rifles were then refurbished and newly overhauled scopes and mounts refitted, each rifle then being collimated to its new scope. He believed that the scopes, mounts and rifles were then supposed to be stamped with the relevant new serial numbers, but he admitted he never did a single one and wasn't sure who, if anyone, ever did. Thus, many No. 4 (T)s will be found with two or three scope numbers, others retain only one and many other marks have subsequently been crossed out, ground off or simply omitted.

Another anomaly is that an unknown number of production rifles had two-groove barrels, and retained them throughout conversion, while the majority of genuine rifles will have been fitted with five-groove barrels. Both types may, or may not bear all of the correct stampings that denote a converted H&H No. 4 (T). Of course, there are still many rifles around today that pre-date 1943, which means that all of the usual H&H inspection marks were never put on, as the full system for marking of components had not, by that date, been finalised. Thus, you will find genuine H&H conversions missing the 'S' or 'TR' stamps, unmarked butts, and no 'T' marks on the left receiver. This is even more common with surviving 1930s' Trials examples, which normally bear absolutely no 'official' markings whatsoever. No. 4 (T) rifles also exist with the correctly specified slab-sided front-sight block, while others retain the earlier pattern and once they had been through various refurbishment programmes, especially in other Commonwealth countries, anything could have happened and often parts or complete rifles can turn up unexpectedly. Many hundreds of genuine No. 32 scopes have been imported from Pakistan in recent years after removal from obsolete sniping rifles. Some collectors and shooters have asserted that any No. 32 scope may be fitted to any No. 4 (T) rifle and simply re-zeroed. On very rare occasions this can work, but generally it does not and very careful setting-up is needed. However, 'careful' is not always an entirely accurate description, as the RSAF armourer previously mentioned told the author that if the malleable-cast-iron mount proved to be a problem, judicious use of a two-pound copper hammer often solved it. Presumably the Holland & Holland gunsmiths would all have had nervous breakdowns if they had known.

The storage chests are still not too hard to find and putting together a convincing Complete Equipment Schedule is quite feasible, but if it is being sold by a local gun dealer at a price that doesn't require you to sell your house first, be very, very wary. Occasionally, a 'sleeper' does emerge from an early collection or even a museum, but normally such rare beasts will be encountered in the catalogues of a large specialist auction house and be offered at a price that will require you to sit down. And never, *ever* believe the provenance story that comes with a rifle, unless it is accompanied by cast-iron documentation. Such paperwork is far rarer than the rifles themselves, as ex-sniping Enfields were sold off by the army into the commercial trade by the hundreds, at a time when they were of little interest to collectors or shooters and values were very low. So naturally, no one was the slighted bit bothered about their past history, after all, who cared? My first one, complete in its chest, was £150, but of course that was then.

To sum-up, the watchword as always is *caveat emptor* and a good rule of thumb to abide by is that if it looks too good to be true, then it probably is.

Appendix 2

Specifications

No. 4 Mk I*
Weight: 8 lb 10 oz
Barrel length: 25.2 in.
Overall length: 44.4 in.
Barrel: 2-groove, 1:10 left-hand twist
Calibre: .303 in.
Magazine: 10 rounds

No. 4 (T)
Weight: 11 lb with scope and mount
Barrel length: 25.2 in.
Overall length: 44.4 in.
Barrel: 5-groove, 1:10 left-hand twist
Calibre: .303 in.
Magazine: 10 rounds

Telescope, Mk III
Length: 11 in.
Weight in mount: 2 lb 2 oz
Objective lens diameter: 19 mm
Ocular lens diameter: 24 mm
Magnification: 3×, fixed focus
Range graduation on drum: 100–1,300 yards
Lateral adjustment on drum: 16–0–16

Mk VII .303-inch Cartridge
Introduced: 1910
Bullet weight: 174 grains, pointed, flat-based bullet
Charge: 37 grains cordite
Muzzle velocity: 2,440 ft/s
Chamber pressure: 42,000 psi

Mk VIIIz .303-inch Cartridge
Introduced: 1938
Bullet weight: 175–190 grains, pointed, boat-tailed bullet
Charge: 38 grains Neonite (nitro-cellulose)
Muzzle velocity: 2,525 ft/s
Chamber pressure: 50,000 psi

.276-inch Enfield Cartridge
Introduced: 1912
Bullet weight: 165 grains, pointed bullet
Charge: 49.3 grains cordite
Muzzle velocity: 2,785 ft/s
Chamber pressure: 80,000–90,000 psi

Notes

Chapter 1: Learning the Trade

1. One ex-sniper from that era told me his unit was always referred to as 'the leper colony' and excluded from almost every regimental event.
2. At age fourteen, to his parents' bemusement he bought and had delivered a huge mahogany bookcase, which his daughter still has.

Chapter 2: Sniper Training and Equipment

1. This was theoretical, some regiments chose to employ more, others less. By 1944 the battalion complement of snipers had been raised to a minimum of sixteen, indicating their importance on the battlefield.
2. More detailed information on this process is given in Appendix 1.
3. Aiming off to left or right to allow the side-wind to drift the bullet onto the target. A hard skill to master.
4. A nickname given to civilian target shooters who lay prone on gravel beds at shooting ranges.
5. Strictly speaking, the term *ghillie* was applicable only to a professional Highland deer-stalker, a group of men who were unrivalled in their skill with the Scout Telescope.
6. A slang term for a ghillie observer.
7. A gathering place for armoured vehicles to be fuelled up and checked before action. From the Dutch South African word *laager*, meaning a camp formed by circling waggons.
8. The objective lens is the furthest away from the shooter and gathers light, while the ocular lens is the closest to the shooter's eye.

9. Harry kept his, but it never recovered from its dousing in the sea on D-Day and he was later issued with a black-faced Omega wristwatch, which he prized and wore for several decades after the war.
10. Introduced in 1944, these were heated by lighting a small fuse with a match or cigarette which in turn lit an internal heating element invented by ICI. They soon became too hot to handle without a cloth and were known to explode violently on occasions.
11. These early rifles were rebuilt at the RSAF, prior to the contract being awarded to Holland & Holland.
12. The low light of pre-dawn or dusk, when the human eye cannot usually discern any detail, but a telescopic sight with its light-gathering properties would enable a sniper to target the unwary.
13. Royal Electrical and Mechanical Engineers, responsible for the care and repair of infantry weapons.
14. 'No. 2' was Harry's applied name, and not to be confused with the 'official' Enfield No. 2 rifle, which was a .22 training weapon.
15. With the muzzle blocked by something suitable, boiling water was poured down the bore. This expanded the steel, loosened fouling and enabled more efficient cleaning.
16. A sound-moderated automatic firearm was something of a paradox as, if it were fired in fully-automatic mode, it destroyed the internal baffles of the suppressor, rendering it useless. To work properly it should only have been fired in single-shot mode!
17. This is the distance from the face of the closed breech of a firearm to the surface in the chamber on which the cartridge case seats. This point usually corresponds to the rim or shoulder of the cartridge case, and affects the insertion depth of the cartridge. *In extremis* it can prevent the bolt from being closed.
18. Commercial Match ammunition is made to extremely high tolerances and is both very accurate and very expensive.
19. The Mk VIIIz cartridge was loaded with a heavier bullet, not recommended for use in infantry rifles.
20. So named after the Dum Dum arsenal in Calcutta, India, which produced expanding lead bullets for hunting in the late nineteenth century. The term gradually became a generic one,

covering any bullet that mushroomed or exploded on impact. They were, and still are, prohibited for use in warfare.
21. A full account appears later.
22. This would appear to be an example of the 'Smock, Camouflaged Windproof' introduced in 1943 which, rather strangely, Harry seemed to be unaware of.
23. Mostly based on Sherman and Cromwell tanks, which were nicknamed 'Rhinos'.
24. Ion Idriess, *The Desert Column*.
25. A modified Churchill tank, introduced in 1944, that had a flame-thrower mounted on the hull, just below the main gun.

Chapter 3: D-Day and Into the *Bocage*

1. The MG 42 machine gun was one of the Germans' most feared infantry weapons. It could be used as a portable MG with bipod, or fitted into a tripod for accurate sustained fire. It had a distinctive sound because of its incredibly high rate of fire of up to 1,200 rounds per minute.
2. CSM S. E. Hollis, 1912–72. 6th Battalion, Green Howards. Awarded the VC, 6 June 1944.
3. In WW1, many German machine guns were manufactured at the Spandau Arsenal and this name stuck, being later applied in WW2 to the MG 34 and MG 42 family of machine guns.
4. The long arm of coincidence also came into play here, when Harry, in Normandy for a D-Day anniversary, had a heart attack and ended up in exactly the same hospital he had been admitted to some fifty years previously.

Chapter 4: Driving Inland

1. APDS is Armour-Piercing Discarding Sabot. This is a projectile with a light outer casing of the same calibre as the gun, but a much smaller diameter heavy tungsten steel armour-piercing core. On firing, the outer casing drops away and the armour-piercing core, still travelling at very high velocity, continues towards the target.
2. Harry thus became probably the only sniper who ever qualified as a 'gun-layer 1st class' on 6-pounder and 17-pounder anti-tank guns. After the war this caused some confusion with his records,

when the Ministry of Defence enquired at what point had he had transferred to the Royal Artillery.
3. Captain P. M. Young, age 24, killed in action 28 June 1944. Buried in St-Manvieu War Cemetery, Cheux.
4. *Shrapnellmine*, *Springmine* or *Splittermine*.
5. The Universal Carrier, better known as the Bren Carrier, was a tracked 3.75-ton lightly armoured vehicle with a range of 150 miles and top speed of 30 mph. It could carry machine guns, anti-tank projectors, 2-inch mortars or be used for ammunition, personnel or evacuating wounded. By 1945 57,000 had been manufactured.
6. The driver of the ambulance was the Chaplain, Captain H. S. G. Thomas, who was awarded the MC for this act.
7. Every batch of ammunition manufactured possessed slightly different physical characteristics, such as variations in charge or bullet weight, and this altered its point of impact. Using a new batch required the rifle to be re-zeroed.
8. Warrant Officer S. Morton, aged 33. Died 26 June 1944. Buried in Bayeux War Cemetery.
9. Tanks quickly become immobile when 'bellied' on tree-stumps and thus sitting ducks for anti-tank infantry.
10. Major P. S. Newton was awarded the Military Cross and Corporal J. Ellis the Distinguished Conduct Medal.
11. Lt. H. D. McNeile, killed in action, 12 September 1944, aged 24. Buried in Sainte Marie Cemetery, Le Havre.

Chapter 5: Belgium and the Netherlands

1. Corporal John William Harper, VC, killed in action, 29 September 1944, aged 28. Buried in Leopoldsburg War Cemetery, Limburg, Belgium.
2. It was a disposable, single-use recoilless rocket launcher firing a cone shaped-charge with a maximum range of no more than 70 yards, but it was highly effective. The smaller version could penetrate 5.5 inches of armour, the later, larger variants almost 8 inches, which was thicker than any British tank armour of the time.
3. The famous American cigarette lighters, often, for want of any safer fuel, filled with petrol/gasoline.

4. 4748330 Pte J. Metcalfe. Awarded the Dutch Order of the Bronze Lion.
5. Named in the War Diary as Major T. Nicholson.
6. Typhoons carried eight RP3 air-to-ground rockets, introduced in 1943. Each had a 60-pound charge with an armour-piercing head and one alone could destroy any existing German tank, frequently blowing even Tiger tanks upside down. They also carried four wing-mounted 20 mm Hispano cannon.
7. Corporal A. Furniss, killed in action, 4 November 1944, aged 25. Buried in Fijnaart-Heiningen Cemetery, Roosendaal, Netherlands.
8. The tune originated, in fact, from *Fra Diavolo*, a comic opera written in 1830 by Daniel Auber. A version of the story later became a popular Laurel and Hardy film of 1933, *The Devil's Brother*.
9. Known in German as the *Westwall*, this was a German defensive line stretching more than 390 miles (630 km) from Kleve on the border of the Netherlands, to the town of Weil am Rhein on the Swiss border. The line comprised almost 20,000 bunkers, with hundreds of tank traps and infantry tunnels.
10. This was a turretless tank, based on a Sherman, Churchill or Canadian Ram chassis, that could hold ten (or more) infantry as well as a couple of powerful .50 calibre Browning heavy machine guns.
11. A Matilda or Sherman tank with a motor-driven drum on the front that had heavy chains fitted. These detonated any mines in its path.
12. This was to avoid placing any pressure on the rifle's wooden furniture and thus the barrel, which would result in poor accuracy.
13. The name was from an acronym: D – Model year 1942, U – Utility, K – All wheel drive, W – Dual axle. Universally known as 'The Duck' it was an American-built, 31-foot, 6.5-ton amphibious transport vehicle, 2,000 of which were supplied to Britain during 1943–45 under Lend-Lease.
14. A Buffalo was a 'Landing Vehicle, Tracked' or LVT, a 26-foot, 18-ton tracked landing craft with a crew of six. Heavily armed with 20 mm cannon or .50 cal. machine guns, some 600 were used during the advance across Holland and Germany.

15. The German front-line defences, situated just beyond the land they had deliberately flooded.
16. For an honest description of civilian life in Arnhem during this time, Audrey Hepburn's account, *The Dutch Girl*, should be read.

Chapter 6: Aftermath and Later Life

1. Harry must be a little confused here. The war against Japan had ended in August 1945, though in 1947 British troops were still part of the Allied Occupation Force in Japan; perhaps Harry's language skills might have been needed there – or alternatively the brigadier might have been trying to send Harry far away to postpone an embarrassing marriage.
2. Harry and Erni had a church wedding in Lüneburg but later had a second civil ceremony in Berlin that a few of Erni's surviving relatives were able to attend. The wedding photograph reproduced in the Plates was taken after the Berlin ceremony.
3. These were: General News Services, Lancashire Press Agency, Yorkshire Press Agency, Midlands Press Agency, Trade and Technical News Services and News Associates.

Appendix 1: The Enfield No. 4 (T) Sniping Rifle

1. Research after 1918 showed that most combats took place at ranges between 20 and 200 yards.
2. But apparently very few from Fazakerly, as they did not meet the accuracy standard.
3. In accuracy tests, there was actually little difference between the five- and two-groove barrels, but the two-groove type wore out and lost precision more quickly than the five-groove.
4. No documentation now exists as to how many were ever produced. Some authorities believe it to be fewer than 200.

Bibliography

Ambrose, Stephen, *D-Day*. Simon & Schuster, New York, 2016
Beevor, Antony, *D-Day*. Penguin, London, 2014
Hesketh-Prichard, Vernon H., *Sniping in France*. Hutchinson, London, 1919
Houghton, Steve, *The British Sniper, A Century of Evolution*. Swift and Bold Publishing, Suffolk, 2018
Idriess, Ion, *The Desert Column*. ETT Imprints, Sydney, 2017
Laidler, Peter, *The .303 No.4 (T) Sniper Rifle*. Greenhill Books, 1993
——, *Telescope Sight No. 32*. DS Books, Kent, 2022
Matzen, Robert, *The Dutch Girl*. Goodknight Books, New York, 2019
Pegler, Martin. *Out of Nowhere*. Osprey Publishing, Oxford, 2004
——, *The Military Sniper since 1914*. Osprey Publishing, Oxford, 2001
Scott, Don. *Polar Bears from Sheffield*. Tiger & Rose Publications, Sheffield, 2001
Sheffield, Major O. F., *The Yorks and Lancs Regiment*, Vol. III. Gale and Polden, Aldershot, 1956
Shore, Captain C., *With British Snipers to the Reich*. Lancer Militaria, Arkansas, 1988
Skennerton, Ian, *British Sniper 1915–1983*. Skennerton Publishing, Labrador, Queensland, 1984
——, *British Empire Sniping Rifles*, Skennerton Publishing, Labrador, Queensland, 2008
Yee, Gary, *World War II Snipers*. Casemate Publishers, Havertown, PA, 2022

Index

XXX Corps 58, 82, 109
49th Division 108, 117, 126, 142
104th US Infantry Division 117

Aarle-Rixtel 112
Alex Martin 22
Aldis P.1918 scope 23
ammunition 6, 23, 28–36, 43, 58, 67, 72–3, 86, 89, 94, 103, 111, 116, 162, 177
anti-tank guns 19, 49, 56, 57, 73, 81, 99, 113, 116, 127, 136
Antwerp–Turnhout Canal 109, 119
Army Film and Photographic Unit (AFPU) 148, 149
Arnhem 108, 128, 134, 135, 139
artillery 10, 14, 18–19, 34, 49, 51, 53, 55–6, 59, 63, 69, 73–4, 79, 82, 89, 93, 97–9, 102, 109, 118, 120, 127, 130–2, 134–5, 139, 147, 171
Audrieu 86

backlash 28, 175
Barbe Farm 82
barrel life 30
Bayeux 58, 76, 85
bayonets 22, 24, 127
binoculars 23, 24, 38, 42, 46, 55, 59, 65, 68, 78, 79, 87, 88, 90, 98, 102, 105, 107, 117, 124, 136, 137, 171
Bisley Camp 9, 12–16
bocage 21, 39, 46, 57, 58, 63, 80, 89, 108, 109
booby traps 112, 115, 127
boots 38, 39, 42, 62, 91, 107, 118
Bouncing Betty 80
Bren gun 23, 26, 46, 53, 65, 80, 81, 82, 84, 88, 89, 100, 101, 105, 121, 125, 145, 146, 150, 163, 171

Bren gun carrier (BGC) 81, 89, 145
Buffalo amphibian 134

Caen 49, 89, 93, 96, 104
camouflage 5, 9, 14, 16, 17, 18, 19, 20, 24, 36–52, 55, 57, 63, 66, 68, 76, 87, 98, 103, 105, 107, 111, 120, 136, 137
Churchill Flail 105, 112, 127, 134
cleaning 22, 24, 25, 30–1, 32, 75, 77, 115, 169
cleaning rods 25, 30
compass 18, 20, 21, 23, 24, 43, 54, 59, 64
Complete Equipment Schedule (CES) 23
Crocodile 56
crosshairs 16, 27

D-Day 7, 20, 24, 31, 39, 49, 58–71, 156, 159
De-bollickers 80
De Hoven 134
deer-stalking 14, 39, 144, 145, 146
Denison smock 31, 40–44, 52, 107
Depôt de Mendicitié 109, 110, 111
Dresden 147
Ducy-Ste-Marguerite 85
DUKW 132, 133, 134
dysentery 44, 62, 76

Eindhoven 112
Ellekon 138
Empire Lance, MS 58
Enfield rifles:
 Short, Magazine Lee Enfield (SMLE) 2, 4
 No. 1 P14.W (T) 2, 22

Index

No. 4 Mk. I 2, 22, 164, 166, 170; *see also* Appendix 2
No. 4(T) rifle No. 2, 21–24, 30, 85, 151; *see also* Appendices 1 & 2
entrenching tool 44

Fairbairn-Sykes knife 14, 23, 24, 45, 48, 127
Falaise 89
First World War (Great War) 1, 6–8, 13, 43, 45, 47, 156
Fontenay-le-Pesnel 72–4
Forêt-de-Brotonne 99
Furness, Erni 147–9, 152, 153, 157, 158, 159
Furniss, Cpl A. 122

German snipers 1, 29, 37, 48, 49, 53, 63, 66, 68, 76, 79, 85, 100, 105, 130
ghillies 14–15, 39
ghillie suit 39
Gold Beach 58
Green Howards (Princess of Wales's Own Yorkshire Regiment) 6, 58, 64, 65, 69, 70
grenades 23, 32, 62, 64, 65, 78, 80, 81, 84, 88, 99, 104, 111, 132

Halford, Lt-Col C. K. 145, 148
Hallamshire Battalion (York and Lancaster Regiment) 70, 93, 96, 106, 111, 115, 110, 119, 122, 123, 125, 126, 133, 136, 138
Harfleur 106
Harper, Cpl. J. W., VC 110
Hart Dyke, Lt. Col. T. 71, 105, 130, 140
helmets 38, 43, 44, 52, 53, 61, 69, 79, 91, 94, 108, 117
Hesketh-Prichard, Capt. V. H. 4, 7
hides 14, 20, 28, 37, 46–9, 52, 55, 72, 81, 87, 90, 111, 117, 118, 124, 128, 129–33, 140
Holland 43, 98, 115, 116, 122, 125, 132, 133, 135, 136, 139

Holland & Holland 25, 31, 165, 167–71, 179
Hollis, Sgt. S., VC 65
Hythe School of Musketry 2, 9, 13, 16, 164

insignia 14, 15, 39, 40, 54, 57, 71, 94, 142
instructors 2, 10, 11, 13, 14, 16, 17, 20, 21, 23, 25, 37, 47–9, 85, 104, 164
Intelligence 9, 10, 14, 15, 18, 19, 46, 53–5, 57, 64, 66, 76, 83, 85, 86, 91–3, 95, 103, 107, 118, 126, 127, 135, 142, 150
International News Photos Agency 154, 155

Kangaroo 127
Kensington's 33, 86, 94
Khyber Factor 14
King's Own Yorkshire Light Infantry (KOYLI) 82

La Cerlangue 106
Landing Craft Assault (LCA) 21, 58, 59
Le Havre 104, 106, 109
Leica 102, 153–5
Lewis machine gun 163
Llanberis Sniper Training School 9, 15, 19–20
Lille 109
Lovat Scouts 15, 16
Lowry, L. S. 153

Maas, River 126
magazines 32, 33, 92
Manchester 3, 5, 71, 131, 154,
Mentioned in Despatches, 124
Merksplas 109
Metcalf, Sniper 118
MG 42 59, 67, 99, 111
mines 24, 80, 81, 114, 121, 126–8, 136
'Moaning Minnie': *see* Nebelwerfer
Mulberry Harbours 73

Nebelwerfer 69

Index

Nijlen 108
Nijmegen 128, 131
No. 32 Telescopic sight 12, 21, 24, 27, 171
  No. 32 Mk. I 172–5; see also Appendix 2
  No. 32 Mk. II 25, 47, 175–6
  No. 32 Mk. III 25, 176
  No. 32 adjuster drums:
    elevation (range) 26, 27, 28, 144, 172–4, 176, 177
    deflection 13, 26, 28, 144, 172, 174, 176,
    Normandy 10, 19, 21, 23, 24, 36, 37, 39, 42, 48, 51, 57, 63, 66, 68, 72, 76, 82, 93, 158, 159

Oudemolen 123

Panther Mk. V 73, 119
Pattern 1907 sling 11, 23, 41, 45, 46, 139
Panzerfaust 113, 114, 116
Panzergrenadiers 63, 72, 114
'Polar Bears' 71
Poussy-la-Campagne 93

rations 24, 33, 75, 96, 106, 117, 142
Regimental Aid Post 76, 95, 142
reticles: see crosshairs
Rhine River 123, 126, 128, 134 120
Rijn River 133
Roosendaal 120, 121, 126
Rotterdam 116
Royal Small Arms Factory (RSAF) 26

Savage No. 4 (T) rifle 25
Scheldt Estuary 116, 117
Scout Regiment Telescope 12, 14, 16, 17, 21, 23, 24, 26, 38, 42, 51, 52, 55, 59, 89, 90, 93, 103, 107, 124, 136, 146, 151,
scrim 37, 38, 39, 42, 43
Siegfried Line 126
Seine River 99, 101, 103
Sherman 111, 112, 114

sight picture 94
Simmil, Capt. 142, 146
slit trench 32, 33, 44, 46, 62, 69, 74–6, 79, 81, 85, 115, 122–3
Spandau: see MG 42
St Leger 58
Sten gun 31, 65, 112, 114, 175
suppressor 35
Sutkus, Gef. Bruno 68

telescopic sights 21–3, 25, 27–9, 34, 38, 66, 78, 90, 137, 139, 140, 161, 171, 172
Tessel Wood 74, 78, 82
'Tommy-cookers' 114
trigger pressure 12
Typhoon fighter-bomber 89, 120, 121, 134

Utrecht 139

Vendes 82
Venlo 126, 127
Versailles Treaty 2
Ver-sur-Mere 58, 62
Vickers machine gun 33, 82, 86, 88, 94, 163
Vieux-Port 101

Waffen-SS 13, 51, 114, 115, 120, 124, 125, 135
Warminster, School of Infantry 151
webbing 23, 24, 42–6, 175
Wetering, canal 130,
Wetering, river 132, 133
Wildermuth, Col. E. 104, 106
wire cage 37
winter smock 43
Wuustwezel 119

Young, Lt. P. M. 74, 75

zeroing 29, 85, 174, 177
Zetten 131, 133
'Zippos' 114